The Polishing Cloth

Seventh Edition

Georgia Perimeter College

Hank Eidson • Tamara Shue • Ted Wadley

Editors

KENDALL/HUNT PUBLISHING COMPANY
4050 Westmark Drive Dubuque, Iowa 52002

Cover artwork by Joanne Bishop

ISBN 0-7872-5115-1

Printed in the United States of America
10 9 8 7 6 5 4 3 2

CONTENTS

Preface

This edition of The Polishing Cloth is a transitional one. Not only is it the first edition to bear the college's new name, but it is also the first edition to use the new course numbers for our semester offerings. However, in the midst of all these changes, many aspects of The Polishing Cloth have remained the same. We still envision this text as an excellent tool to help both students and teachers, and we still believe in the pedagogical value of good student writing examples. We realize that students do not write in a vacuum and, therefore, need good examples to emulate. Consequently, we, as the editors before us, have tried to pick the best and most useful examples of student work from the numerous submissions we have received.

As a result of this painstaking selection process, this edition contains several examples of different rhetorical models. We have attempted to cover as many of the different modes as possible, but we realize that certain rhetorical strategies are taught more often than others. We also understand that many of the essays that we have classified as a specific rhetorical mode can be used to illustrate elements of other rhetorical categories. Even though we have tried to arrange the text in a manner that will be helpful to our readers, we hope that different instructors and students will find their own methods for using the fine examples of student writing in this text. In addition, we hope that the use of the semester course numbers will help students identify appropriate assignments. The only numbers not changed are those for the ENSL courses. We have not altered these numbers because significant changes have been made in the ENSL course offerings due to semester conversion. Therefore, we did not have corresponding numbers for the new ENSL courses. Nevertheless, we have tried our best to make this edition as easy to use and accessible as possible.

Another area of concern for the editors, past and present, has been the proofing and editing of student work. Although we have made the necessary grammatical and mechanical changes, we have tried to alter the students' papers as little as possible. We believe that much can be gained from both the successes and foibles of student writers; therefore, readers may find elements that they would modify, just as readers do with all writing. However, even with these minor alterations, we have attempted to keep the tone and content of all of our students' submissions.

The editors of this edition have many people to thank. We first must extend our sincere appreciation to all of the students and teachers who submitted works for consideration. We have been quite pleased and surprised with the overwhelming number of submissions this year. Also, we would like to thank Margee Bright-Ragland for her help in locating student artwork to brighten this edition and Sandra Rosseter and the Instructional Support staff on all campuses for their help in locating excellent examples of actual Regents' essay exams. We would also like to express our appreciation to David Tart of Kendall/Hunt Publishing for his diligence and patience throughout the process of putting this edition together. These individuals have made our job much easier and more enjoyable.

Finally, we would like to thank Georgia Perimeter College President Jacquelyn Belcher for her continued encouragement and support. We also wish to thank Vice-Presidents Myrtle Dorsey and Linda Exley for the administrative support that helps keep such a major project moving forward. In addition, we want to thank Dean Ron Swofford and the members of Literary Publications Executive Board for their intelligent advice and guidance. Even though we have tried to thank several people, we realize that there are countless others at the college whose time and effort have added to the success of The Polishing Cloth. We hope that they know how grateful we are for the opportunity to work with such committed and competent educators.

Dunwoody, Georgia
April 8, 1998
Hank Eidson
Tamara Shue
Ted Wadley

The Polishing Cloth Editorial Board

Literary Publications Executive Board

List of Contributors of Artwork

The Polishing Cloth

The following editions are collected at the Dunwoody Campus Library.

Vol. 1, No. 1	Spring, 1985
Vol. 1, No. 2	Fall and Winter, 1985-1986
Vol. 2, No. 1	Spring and Summer, 1985-1986
Vol. 2, No. 2	Fall and Winter, 1986-1987
Vol. 3, No, 1	Spring and Summer, 1986-1987
Vol. 3, No. 2	Fall and Winter, 1987-1988
Vol. 4, No. 1	Spring and Summer, 1988
Vol. 5	1988-1989
Vol. 6	1990
Vol. 7	1991
First Edition	1992
Second Edition	1993
Third Edition	1994
Fourth Edition	1995
Fifth Edition	1996
Sixth Edition	1997
Seventh Edition	1998

My Room

Alma Mujikanovic

ENSL 017/Description

I am a person who never fully belongs to one time or place. In fact, I like many different places, events, or seasons. Usually, my favorite place to spend free time and relax would be outside on the top of a mountain. Just recently, I discovered one small quiet place that has been there forever, but I had never paid close attention to it before. The place I am talking about is my room.

My room is one of three rooms in my apartment. If I had to describe it with just one word, I think that word would be simple. As soon as you walk in, you would notice that its size is too small for two people to share. However, my sister and I would never complain about it because we know that affording something better is impossible. The floor is covered with carpet that has a very unusual color. There is just one window that hardly opens and closes with blinds on it. Because of the small amount of light we have in the room, my sister and I decorated the window with plain white curtains.

Next to the window are two beds that my sister and I placed side by side in order to save some space. Our beds are covered with a very beautiful and unusual quilt that is handmade. The quilt was made for my sister and me, and it is called "a cover of support and friendship." We got it as a present just recently from an agency as a sign of appreciation for our work with them. It is divided into thirty squares, and each square has a handmade design, and above it the name of the woman who made the square. All the squares are connected, giving a beautiful and warm cover for us. Besides beds, there are just a few more things in the room: two small tables, one desk with a computer on it, a bookshelf, a mirror, and two lamps. The closet, where we keep our clothes, is somehow separate from this small world. The bookshelf contains several books, including The Diary of Anne Frank. All the books I have I received as presents from my friends. I find myself reading them on long and dark nights when I cannot sleep. A small table that sits to the side of my bed holds the phone and a lamp on it. On the other one we put a printer.

One small detail that decorates my room is a medium-sized picture that my best friend gave me. This picture reminds me of my home and my "life" which is constructed just from the letters. The atmosphere of my room is very warm. Small details in it are simple, but they are valuable to me. The room always smells of my favorite perfume, and it makes me feel welcomed and comfortable. My sister and I try to keep it clean and well-organized even when it looks "bleak" sometimes. My favorite thing to do is to sit on my bed with a cup of warm coffee and read books. After reading for a long time, I turn around and look. "Just simple things make life;" I am quietly thinking and realizing that my large and fashionable room in my home in Bosnia has been replaced by this one. However, this one is O.K., and most importantly, it has a healthy atmosphere

My room is quiet and simple--like me. It does not have anything valuable in it, but it is very valuable to me. I like to be there when I am happy, disappointed, sad, or homesick. It makes me feel free and comfortable while taking new steps in my life. My room has become one of my favorite places.

♦♦♦

"How can I know what I think
till I see what I say?"

E. M. Forster

My Friend's Computer Room

Andy Parker

English 0098/Descriptive Paragraph

Whenever I go to my friend's, I always pass his computer room before getting to his bedroom. Yesterday I noticed how unsanitary it really is. It looks as if it has not been cleaned in years. There are urine stains on the carpet from the animals; they seem to think that it is a huge litter box. The smell is sometimes unbearable, but I have gotten accustomed to it. Old broken microwaves, newspapers, shoes without a match, and dead dried-out plants are a few of the items that are scattered around the room. Dust seems to find its way to my nose whenever the ceiling fan is on, and cobwebs have collected in each corner of the room. Whenever something is broken, it is placed on the floor to rot or to make an indention in the floor. Consequently, I think it looks like a garage with carpet. The only thing that is missing is a broken down motorcycle and a lawnmower. This room should be cleaned out with a bulldozer and redecorated all over again. Whenever I have my own house, it will definitely not have any rooms that resemble this one.

♦♦♦

"Language most shows a man; speak that I may see thee."

Ben Jonson

My Sony Playstation

Robert Benjamin

English 0099/Description

In today's society, electronics play an enormous role. Almost every American has a computer or some sort of electronic device. A year ago, Sony produced a new playing device named the Sony Playstation. Because of its petite size, great graphics, and high cost, my Sony Playstation is the primary thing I would try to save in a fire.

An important reason for saving the Sony Playstation is its petite size. It is shaped in a small square and has two circular buttons on the face that open and close the CD-Rom. This allows the user to load games into the unit in the simplest manner possible. The memory card is a little chip that is the size of a pen cap and fits into the front of the Playstation. These features allow for the unit to take up only a very small space in a person's house. The Playstation is also easy to install. A simple connecting wire runs into the back of any cable-ready television, and the connection to the television takes only a few seconds. With its compact size and ease of hookup, the Sony Playstation could be easily grabbed and removed in case of fire.

Another reason for rescuing my Sony Playstation is the unbelievable graphics. Sony made sure that when the Playstation was developed the graphics would be as realistic as possible. When playing sports games such as John Madden's Football '98 or Gameday '98, the visual imagery is almost equal to virtual reality. I feel as if I am playing in the game itself. When a player makes a tackle, one can hear the sounds of the helmets cracking, pads pounding, and bodies smashing. Sony recently introduced a game called Resident Evil 2. This is an action packed game where a cop must kill all the zombies in town. The visual imagery of blood squirting out of zombies as their heads are ripped from their bodies can leave a person speechless. The graphics help make the Sony Playstation incredibly enjoyable. For this reason, I would save it from a fire.

A final important reason why I would save the Sony Playstation from a fire is its high price. Last year Sony priced its Playstation at two hundred dollars. That was an enormous expense for any game-playing device. I waited a couple of months to purchase this item in hopes that the price would decline with time. Unfortunately, because the item has been tremendously popular, the price never decreased. Therefore, I decided to go ahead and purchase the item. As I was discussing my purchase with a store salesperson, I discovered that I needed a memory card, another controller, and additional games. All of these items are optional with the Sony Playstation. However, the cost of these additional features and games raised the overall price to almost four hundred dollars. The games by themselves cost anywhere from fifty to sixty dollars a piece. Until that day, I have never spent four hundred dollars anywhere. Obviously, my Sony Playstation is my prize possession. I will always make sure that wherever I go, my four hundred-dollar device will follow.

A person's natural response in case of a fire is to get out as quickly as possible. Often we try to grab something that we value when escaping. Typically, this item is either very expensive or highly cherished. In case of a fire, I would try to take something that not only has a high dollar value but also provides a great deal of enjoyment. It would also be important to take this item in as quick a manner as possible. Because it is extremely expensive, highly enjoyable due to its great graphics, and easily removed, my Sony Playstation is the one item I would save in case of a fire.

◆◆◆

Patchwork

Laura Judy

English 1101/Description

An ancient, faded patchwork quilt covers the chest, concealing its innards in place of the lid which has long since disappeared. Each square of the quilt contains a carefully stitched remnant of my grandmother's life. The gentle seams between the pictures bind together her memories, keeping them safe for future generations. With great care, I lift aside the soft, heavy quilt and begin to discover some of the treasures which my grandmother held so dear.

First, I pull out a dust-covered shoebox and gently lift its lid. When a cloud of dust wafts into my nose, I sneeze. Inside the box, I discover a variety of seashells of many different sizes. Leaning closer to the box, I can still smell the salty, airy scent of the sea mixed with the dust on them. Delighted, I lift a large conch shell to my ear and listen to the gentle, roaring sounds of the sea, just as my grandmother taught me to do years ago. I replace the lid on the shoebox with a smile and continue to search for treasures in the old wooden chest.

An old-fashioned Coca-Cola bottle nestled among some clothing catches my eye. Nothing like the cans of today, this bottle is clear and beautiful. Inspecting it more closely, I can see my reflection in it, distorted by the shape of the glass. With a smile, I imagine my young grandmother sitting on her white wicker porch swing with the bottle in her hand. I gently place it back into the chest, making sure that it does not break.

The next item I pick up is a baseball. I carefully run my fingers over the hard, brown leather stitching and imagine that I can hear the sounds of an old-fashioned baseball game. With cheers ringing in my ears, I softly return the baseball to the chest and move on to the next treasure.

The last item that I pick up from the chest, stuck in the same old, musty clothing and yellowed newspapers, is a small doll. Its hair, once blond, is now tangled and dirty, and the dress that had been pure white is now an odd brown color. I cradle the doll, however, comforted by the thought that my grandmother had once spent long hours playing outside in the dirt with her precious toy. Before placing it back into the chest, I wrap the doll carefully in a green sweater decorated with flowers.

A smile brushes my lips as I touch each of the old treasures and remember my grandmother. Lifting the precious quilt from where I had set it on the table, I gently return it to the top of the chest. I note that four of the pictures on the quilt depict a seashell, a glass bottle, a baseball, and a doll. With a calm smile, I turn to walk up the stairs, taking the peaceful memory of my grandmother with me, secure in the fact that I know her better now.

◆◆◆

"Words:
the only thing that lasts forever."

William Hazlitt

A Familiar Sight

Huy D. Nguyen

English 1101/Description

Wandering the campus, I try to find a sight that triggers my interest. Unconsciously, my feet bring me to a familiar sight that I drive by almost every day. Ironically, the familiarity of the place stops me and captures my attention. It is a part of the soccer field next to Parking Lot #6. The soccer field doesn't attract me at all, for it is a monotonous and plain scene. What really catches my eye is the other side of the road. The extraordinary diversity of plants and structures mesmerizes me and helps me relate to the natural world.

Being fascinated by what I have never actually appreciated, I am at first motionless before such beauty. A January breeze creeps inside my coat, caressing me with its icy fingers as if it is reminding me that winter has truly arrived. The frigid cold has frozen everything, including dirty particles in the atmosphere, leaving behind the genuine purity of the air. A gentle wind touches the tops of all the tall pine trees in the far background. It makes them sway rhythmically like a band of lilting singers in a chorus. Even in cold weather, the pine trees yield a greenish color, denoting a healthiness that most other trees do not possess. Pine trees do not grow to the size of oaks, horse chestnuts, or maples. In fact, they are slim and tall, but their spirit of survival is admirable. They are one of the few species that can thrive in the harshest conditions that Mother Nature imposes on living things. And here they stand, decorating the scene with their original green.

Next, I notice that down on the bottom, untouched by humans, thick scrubs competitively inhabit the ground. Unlike our trimmed backyards or tidy gardens, here small trees and bushes grow in a genuinely natural condition. The struggle for life is highly intense, and the competitive spirit is truly alive. Trees seem to have a generous philosophy. When the smaller and weaker trees are losing the battle, they give themselves up to the soil. Their dying bodies create a grayish texture on the ground. It is the color of death, but it also promises riches and fertility for the soil so that the other trees, the "winners," can be healthier.

Then, closer to the road, dry pine needles, yellow leaves, and a row of trees tell me a story of a family. Their withered appearances create a false impression of the lifelessness of the winter. Little do we know that their lives do not cease to exist. They actually take a rest, so they can be ready for the vigorous spring. And here in front of me, the cycle of life is revolving. The brownish yellow leaves are sacrificing themselves to make a better world for their new generation in the spring to come. Their bodies carpet the sidewalk and reflect the rich golden color of the sun. And the straight row of trees next to the road is the row of defenders guarding the natural world a few yards away. They all have interesting shapes and sizes, but the one right in front of me fascinates me the most because of its unusual build. It branches out at the very bottom. The eight gigantic trunks, relatively equal in size, aim at the sky in different directions. Reaching up as high as other trees, the trunks start to branch out themselves. Different branches reach higher to the sky and farther away from one another. I wonder if one day the leaves from the top look down to the leaves closer to the bottom and know that they are relatives and that they share the same roots.

Finally, I am brought back to reality by a passing mechanical monster. Its speed and noise mercilessly stab the peaceful silence. All of a sudden, I realize that it has never been completely silent. The ugly, monotonous sound of car engines in the background invades the air. The little natural world in front of me is surrounded by the not-so-natural one. Where can I find peace in this rushing world? Where can the little trees find peace in their competitive world? Humans and trees are destined for different worlds, yet both worlds require us to compete, sacrifice, and survive.

◆ ◆ ◆

"I am convinced more and more day by day
that fine writing is next to fine doing,
the top thing in the world."

John Keats

Humans on the Moon

Rosanna Yeh

English 1101/Description

Humans have lived on the moon since 1985 when the transporter *Civilization 1* sent five families to experience and survive in the moon's conditions. Since then, the population of the moon has grown steadily to a thriving community of five thousand families.

After man first landed on the moon in 1969, technology on this planet exploded. Scientists fervently labored to invent ways for humans to survive in the moon's atmosphere and harsh weather fluctuations. Many experts thought engineers could build a gigantic geodesic dome so that scientists could control the temperature on the moon; however, after the tragic collapse of an experimental dome in 1978, in which twenty-two workers perished, that theory was quickly abandoned.

A few years later, Dr. Alfred H. Greene developed AIR (Atmosphere Insufficiency Regulator), which creates a livable atmosphere without the use of an expensive dome for cover. AIR makes it possible for the entire surface of the moon to be inhabited so that not just a select few are under the dome. Other scientists have updated AIR, but Dr. Greene is still credited with making the crater-filled, cold, luminous rock livable for humans.

Once an atmosphere had been established, NASA launched several astronauts to the moon so that they could build and modify the moon's landscape for living. They brought not only wood and other building materials but also moon carpet. This lab-developed moss grows well in the moon's soil and will eventually cover most parts of the moon. Moon carpet will provide pure oxygen and a soft, springy, grass-like surface that the inhabitants can frolic over freely without harm, an improvement over the first batch of moon carpet which turned human feet a deep emerald green that faded slowly within a year's time. Scientists are still attempting to develop lunar trees but have only been able to grow bluish but scraggy shrubs that wither in four days.

It took the astronauts three years to complete several buildings, including a main tower to overlook activity and the sprawling living quarters. In the meantime, scientists on earth prepared and trained, through various tests and scenario simulations, several carefully selected families who would live on the moon. NASA taught these families everything from growing moon carpet to fixing AIR, should it malfunction. The youngest member of *Civilization 1* was a slight, almost fairy-like but strong eighteen-year-old female from India, and the oldest member was a towering forty-two-year-old male engineer from Germany. While the families were there, various scientists, doctors, psychologists, and technicians observed each member extensively for his or her reaction to the AIR environment as well as for his or her technical ability and overall physical and emotional well-being. Observations included what time the subject ate, how the subject felt, when the subject relaxed, where the subject went, and how the subject slept. Someone was always present to observe his or her every move.

Not everyone stuck with the experiment. Tom Press, a thirty-six-year-old male, left after two months, declaring he could not stand to look at the "black nothingness out there that sucks you into its endless void, leaving you a shell of a human being." He also complained about "the ubiquitous eyes" of the scientists. However, others disregarded the omnipresent scientists and enthusiastically embraced the clean air, softly carpeted hills and craters, and utopian lifestyle. "The clean air cut right through me like a knife in my blood, and I can almost feel my body being purged of all the pollutants and nastiness of earth. I feel like I'm being reborn into a perfect world," rhapsodized Connie Davids, a twenty-four-year-old member of *Civilization 1*.

The moon has become an ideal haven for many who enjoy clean living despite the rigorous tests and persistent observations of scientists and doctors. Some people have said that our world is gone as we know it and that man has attempted to recreate on the moon our beginning when man was innocent. Some people realize that they are witnessing a great technological advancement that brings them back to the beginning of time when the earth was new and fresh like a newborn baby and that provides them a place where man now can find solace from that broken planet.

◆◆◆

"The original writer is not he who refrains from imitating others, but he who can be imitated by none."

Chateaubriand

A Life in and out of Hell

Adis Bojcic

ENSL 017/Narration

I will never forget April of 1992 when the war in Bosnia began. I played soccer, tennis, basketball, and anything else that was interesting with my friends in the streets and parks. We were just young, naïve fourteen-year-old kids. Still we could feel the pressure in the air, the fear, and the rebellion against the occupation that had lasted for half a century. We thought whatever happened would be over in a couple of days. Nobody thought the war was going to happen. There might be a little fighting, but nothing serious, like in Iraq at the time. Well, that was what my family thought, too. Just like most people, we never went to get all of our savings from the bank. However, after the Serbian Army was kicked out of the city, we found out that all our belongings were destroyed, our house was burned, and all of our savings from the bank were gone, so we were broke and without a home.

When the Yugoslav People's Army, later known as the Serbians or Chechnyans, started bringing extra tanks, weapons, and personnel, the citizens thought it was just a military display. We said, "Maybe the politicians are just playing games; they are trying to scare us; they will not shoot. They will find the way out of this crisis peacefully." But when the army started positioning the personnel and weaponry in strategic hills around the city, we sensed the trouble. That was still not good enough to persuade the people to get their important things to a safe place. My parents acted normally, except they bought extra food and accessories for the house. We thought, "Even if the fighting starts, the Serbs would never be able to enter the city." The citizens tried to arm themselves, but it was too late. On April 4, Serbs took seventy percent of the country and half of my city. Unfortunately, my house was on the occupied side with all of my pictures, clothes, and other belongings.

As the fighting continued to get worse, the Serbs shelled and destroyed as much as they could. My father joined the newly formed Bosnian Army and found a temporary place for us to live on the west side. The Serbs stormed so fast that we did not have time to take anything from the house but a few clothes. All we had time for was to run to the west side while the Bosnian Army tried to hold the Serbs away. We still thought and hoped that we would be back to our home soon, in no longer than a couple of weeks. Finally, the east side was finally liberated, and we were back, but after two and a half months.

The cheering and celebrations replaced the fighting and killing, at least within the city. The question of the day was when we were going to be able to return to our homes. The soldiers had to clean all the land mines, and the engineers had to put up temporary bridges so we could cross the river. All but one bridge was destroyed in the fighting. We knew that we had lost our savings; however, we hoped the house was still safe and whole.

In the middle of June we went back to our "original" side, the east side of the city. As we crossed the newly constructed bridge, all we saw were burned and destroyed houses, buildings, and stores. Our house was still there, standing, but burned. I could not imagine that I would be standing in front of something that appeared so empty, black, and full of sorrow. It was the place where I was born and where I spent most of my childhood. Our happy home gave the impression of all the tragic moments that my city and country were going through at the time. It cried, "Why? Why? Why?"

We stood there without any motion. Using no words, we communicated telepathically. "We could have been out of these troubles and somewhere safe. We could have saved at least the pictures--anything." The same thoughts ran through our minds like wild: "If we had only known!" In those couple of months of war, I had a feeling that I grew more than in the past several years. I understood what happened, only it was bothering me too much. I saw what I should not see; I saw what I had seen only on TV in World War II and Vietnam movies.

Finally, we left the house after almost half a day of trying to comprehend that we had lost everything. But life goes on, and we knew it. I had failed to see what was coming even though it was in front of my eyes. The Serbs had clearly warned us with their actions and behavior. Their actions screamed at us, "You will not exist; we will destroy you!" We could not hear while trying to be pacifists and believing in peace and love. Therefore, I failed to save my memories, my pictures, my clothes, and my videos. Ironically, I took only what was necessary to survive for a week while I escaped, so for the next year I had to stick with what I had.

All of the things that happened in the war taught me valuable lessons. From now on, I will have my documents and pictures ready for whatever happens. I will always try to do my best to see what is coming in the future by looking at today's actions. Probably the most valuable lesson I have learned is never to trust the Serbs and the Croats again. We forgot what they did to us in World War II and how many people died. Now it has happened again, but this time it will not be forgotten. I will return one day to my country, and then I will be ready to fight and defend my home and family with God's help.

◆◆◆

"If you would be a reader, read; if a writer, write."

Epictetus

Why I Don't Like Winter Anymore

Bemir Mehmedbasic

ENSL 017/Narration

I remember winter made me happy when I was a young boy. My excitement about the winter would start early in November with the first signs of cold weather. The first thing that I used to do after waking up was to go to the window and check to see if it was snowing. There were so many beautiful things that we, the children in Sarajevo, used to do during the winter. Building snow houses, snow castles, and snowmen was such a joy. As I got older, most of my time during the winter was spent skiing in the mountains. Climbing up the mountain and then skiing down, those were moments that I wanted never to end. But something happened a few years ago that made me completely change my ideas about the winter.

The war broke out in my country five years ago. Our nice and comfortable life suddenly turned into a real horror. Sarajevo, the city where I lived, was under siege from the very beginning of the war. The siege brought constant bombing of the city, sniper attacks, and death for many citizens. There was no water supply; in addition, both gas and electricity were cut off. There was no wood for stoves. It was impossible to heat the apartment with the electric heater when there was no electricity. It was impossible to cook when there was no way to burn the fire. It was getting almost impossible to survive, especially during winter days. The standard of life that we had before the war, the standard similar to that in developed European countries, became as low as it was centuries ago. The people weren't prepared.

My family and I experienced four terrible winters in Sarajevo that I will never forget. What happened during this time made me completely change my feelings about the winter. I remember how we were freezing in our apartment at temperatures often less than 20°C below zero. It seemed to be warmer out in the snow than in the ice-cold apartment. We couldn't heat up the apartment because there was no power available. We had to sleep with our jackets, boots, and hats on. We had to walk a long way, under the constant threat of shelling and sniper fire, to get water. We had to carry the water all the way because there was no transportation. I will never forget my mother, father, and brother, struggling with canisters of water on a deadly path between our home and the well. Once we got the water home, it was difficult to use it because it froze due to the extremely low temperatures. We had to burn most of our books and furniture to get some fire to heat the water.

Since I was a soldier, there were many other difficult situations for me in the army. Sometimes I had to stay out in snow and ice for more than 24 hours. There was no way to heat my cold feet. The skin on my face and on my hands was rough and severely damaged because of constant exposure to the cold. Very often I was unable to move my fingers because my hands were so cold. I remember a few of my friends dying because they were so exhausted and fell asleep in the snow. Many of these memories I try not to recall, and I feel cold again whenever I think about what happened to me during that time.

I feel I will never again like winter as I used to before the war. The nice things that happened to me during the seventeen years before the war have almost disappeared from my memory, and the terrible memories associated with winter keep coming back even though I try to forget them. Therefore, my feelings about winter will never be the same. I don't get excited about the snow, nor do I think about skiing as I used to before the war. The things that are in my mind now are sunny beaches and blue seas.

◆◆◆

The First Time I Lost Someone I Loved

Manuela Saramondi

ENSL 017/Narration

Vittorio Saramondi was the youngest of twelve children. Vito, what we used to call him, was my father's brother. At the age of forty, he left us because of a deadly disease. He was one victim of cancer that every year kills millions of people around the world. It was the first time in my life that I experienced the pain and the sense of injustice of having someone whom I loved sick.

Every time I hear about this disease, I have a flashback where I picture my uncle. He was tall and athletic. He did not smoke, drink, or use drugs. Nevertheless, he was only thirty-nine years old when he was diagnosed with cancer in his stomach. When I received the news of his illness, I was only fifteen years old, and I could not believe that this kind of injustice had to happen in my family. I remember spending nights praying and hoping for his quick recovery. I cried often and hoped that my prayers would help him and his family. Vito, at that time, was married, and he had two children who needed him. The children were Antonella, who was fourteen years old, and Roberto, who was seven years old. After the diagnosis, for a couple of months Vito tried to live a normal life in spite of his sickness; however, while the days were passing, his body was deteriorating, so he had to go to the hospital.

It was when my uncle was at the hospital that I realized the gravity of his sickness. There, I also started to experience the pain of my uncle's sickness. It was curious how my parents and my relatives thought that they were the most affected by this event and that all of us children were not affected by it as they were. The fact was that they were absolutely wrong because my uncle's illness, particularly while he was in the hospital, deeply marked me. He was in the hospital for a couple of months in a room by himself. It was a white-gray room that gave me a sense of sadness every time I entered. I felt sad not only because I knew Vito was sick but also because the colors that were surrounding my uncle's life were sad; therefore, his wife and he decided to go back home to wait for his departure that was not far away.

Vito stayed home a couple of days before departing this life. The day before his death, I visited him in his house. He was lying down in his king-sized bed. He was feeling comfortable there. The colors of the environment that surrounded him were warmer than in the hospital room. Though he knew he was home because nothing else could help him stay alive, he was relieved to be there. When he saw me, he made me promise to take care of myself and not to worry about him. I could not believe that he was going to die and he was worried about me. The day after our conversation, his daughter Antonella entered through the door in my house and told me he had died. Her words astonished me. Then, even though I was in a lot of pain, I felt almost relieved that he had finally finished suffering.

So many people in the world are affected by this deadly disease, and there are others who are suffering from watching their family members fighting for their lives. Every time I hear about cancer, I remember my Vito and what he passed through. I loved my uncle, and I still love him. I think his young death was a big injustice. I think he didn't deserve it just as nobody deserves to die from this disease. This is why I hope that a cure will come soon so that in the future, no other family has to experience the pain that cancer brings.

An Eventful Day at Zoo Atlanta

Alfonzo C. Ford, II

English 0098/Narration

I am an avid reptile hobbyist and spend much of my free time searching for a new and unusual reptile to see. I cannot afford to travel to the nearest tropical rainforest or go on an African safari adventure. Therefore, I have to visit different pet stores in the metro Atlanta area to attempt to satisfy my passion for viewing reptiles. Unfortunately, pet stores do not offer a large variety of species due to the small market for reptiles in the area. I sometimes find that I have driven twenty-five miles only to find that the reptile selection is no better than the pet store near my house. This is not a good feeling. However, I have found a local place that houses a variety of reptiles, Zoo Atlanta.

Being a student, I find my free time and gas to be very limited. Therefore, I find the Reptile House, located inside Zoo Atlanta, to be the place where I go to satisfy my passion for reptiles. The Reptile House is a warehouse-style building with a greenhouse on both sides. Inside visitors find a large collection of snakes, skinks, chameleons, monitors, dragons, and frogs, all displayed in terrariums duplicating the natural living environments of the species within. In the greenhouses, I can see various reptile species coexisting in a beautiful setting, decorated with green foliage. After spending nearly two hours viewing the fascinating creatures of the Reptile House, I still have time to take in some other animal exhibits at the zoo.

The Ford African Rainforest, which is another exhibit at Zoo Atlanta, offers a collection of different rainforest dwellings for birds and animals from the seven continents of the world. I can see beautiful parrots in an array of colors, flying free in their large aviaries. The Ford African Rainforest is a great place to see monkeys and apes swinging from trees, laughing and playing, just as they do in the wild. When I visit the zoo, I cannot believe the striking resemblance that these primates have to humans. Due to Zoo Atlanta's involvement in the Endangered Species Reproduction Program, I can see a newborn Silver Back Gorilla being nursed by its mother. The zoo's involvement in the Endangered Species Reproduction Program allows endangered species to be bred in captivity, thus adding more life to the zoo without taking from nature. I wish the zoo the best of luck with this program.

While visiting the zoo, I notice that it is committed to the education of the public about animals. There are always zoo personnel speaking about the many animals cared for by the zoo. Besides these speakers, there are educational seminars held on a regular basis. I think it is great to find that the friendly zoo staff is willing to answer all of my questions about animals and their behavior.

I initially went to the zoo to visit just the Reptile House, but as I journeyed through the zoo, I noticed that Zoo Atlanta offered so much more than animals. I believe that my trips to Zoo Atlanta are truly serendipitous. Zoo Atlanta is a great place to go for an educational, get-back-to-nature experience.

◆ ◆ ◆

"Writers are the engineers of human souls."

Joseph Stalin

Until Death Do Us Part

Jim Wilson

English 0099/Narration

In November 1982, on a cool sunny Sunday in a southern Alabama city, Hell came to visit. It was on that day when I realized the true meaning of domestic violence. It was also on this day when I first began to realize how cruel life can be. I don't know how a day that was so perfect could go so wrong. The sky was a brilliant blue and so clear that it seemed I could see right into heaven. There was a cool breeze blowing, but it was not too cold. It was a perfect day, or so I thought. Then all of a sudden, the sky seemed to turn an ashen gray, and the air became hot. Hell had come to earth on that sunny Sunday. The meaning of "until death do us part" was about to become reality.

I was twenty-two years old, and I had not been long out of the city Police Academy. I was still uncertain and afraid of the unknown. I had never experienced what was about to happen, and my partner was about the same. He had not been on the street long; therefore, he was also uncertain. What we were about to experience would shock us both.

At about three o-clock in the afternoon the call came in. The police dispatcher came over the radio and said, "A man with a gun is chasing a woman down the street." All of a sudden the mood changed from relaxed and carefree to tense with fear. The unknown scared me the most. Not knowing what was going to happen next made my heart pump. There was something very strange about this call. It was not typical for this neighborhood. We were responding to a quiet middle-class neighborhood where not much ever happened, especially nothing like this.

As we were racing toward the neighborhood, the dispatcher came over the radio again to give us more information. The dispatcher said, "Shots have been fired, and the woman is down." The radio crackled as police supervisors and other officers acknowledged that they also were en route to the scene. My heart was really pounding now, so hard I thought it was coming out of my chest. I began to realize that this was really happening, and I was about to be thrust right into the middle of it!

We finally arrived, and my worst nightmare had come true. It was not a prank call as I had hoped it would be all the way there. The first thing I noticed was people wandering around the street crying and in a daze as if they had seen the devil himself. The look on their faces was one I would never forget as long as I live.

Then I saw her! A woman was lying face down in the grass on a lawn near me. She was not moving, and I could see why. She was missing the back of her head. It was a mangled mess. And the organ that had once controlled her body was now splattered onto the lawn and matted in her hair. It was a gruesome sight. I had never seen anything like it before, and for a brief moment I was frozen and could not move.

Then suddenly it got worse as I now saw a man lying down on another lawn nearby. He was moving slightly and making a horrible noise. I walked cautiously closer, and as I drew near, I could hear him gasping for breath. When I got close enough to see his face, I realized this sight was even worse than the woman I had just seen. This man had apparently tried to take his own life by putting a shotgun to his face and pulling the trigger, but he had been unsuccessful. The blast did not kill him, but it did remove his face from just below his eyes down into his throat. He was moving his eyes rapidly back and forth as if he were trying to say something. He was gasping for every breath as he gagged on his own blood, which was filling his throat. Thank God the paramedics got there when they did.

Now it was time to try to find out what had happened. I found a woman in the crowd of people who had witnessed the whole ordeal. The woman, who was a neighbor of the dead woman, said her neighbor had been going through a divorce. She explained that the divorce papers had been finalized that day, and apparently the man who was now the ex-husband was very angry. The ex-husband came over to kill his ex-wife and then himself.

The man had succeeded in killing his wife, but he had failed at ending his own life. He now lay on the ground not only horribly wounded and in great pain, but he also had to live with what he had done. The woman had desperately tried to escape the violence of a bad marriage, yet it was her escape that enraged her husband so much that he killed her. He apparently could not live with the thought of being apart from her. I wondered if he thought that if they were both dead, they would be together forever.

My life would be changed forever after that day, for I knew now just how cruel the world could be. I would never look at life the same again. Now my heart pounds harder when I get a call like this because I know the cruel realities are endless.

The reality is that most women who are murdered are killed by their own husbands. They are killed by the very people who vowed their love for them and vowed to protect them "until death do us part." I have asked myself the same question over and over again. How can a man become so angry, so enraged, or so crazy that he would kill the woman he once said he would love and protect forever? How could something so horrible possibly become reality?

My Piercing Experience

Billy Cowart

English 101/Narration

I was determined to get some part of my body pierced. For a while, I wondered if I had what it took to be pierced. I'd never done anything without asking my parents for their permission. Was I ready? That question kept popping up in my head. However, the real tests would be finding the strength to have it done and dealing with the aftermath, including my parents.

While standing outside the "all-in-one" store called Urban Tribe, I argued with myself about getting pierced. Opening the door was the hardest step. I walked into the store, or should I say pushed my way in, and instantly loud music assaulted my ears like an exploding Howitzer. Smoke filled the room giving it an eerie effect, almost tribal. Walls decorated with abstract and junk art attempted to cover up the peeling paint, and clothes that were for sale were thrown in piles, making it hard to find anything. The smell of rubbing alcohol mixed with sweat and perfume assaulted my senses. Go-Go dancers wearing platform shoes and raincoats danced on top of the speakers. This "all-in-one" store had everything, tattooing, shaving, piercing, music, and clothes. I tried to blend in, but I stuck out like a sore thumb or like someone who had just walked from Kansas into the Twilight Zone. The crowd, on the other hand, was busy shopping, dancing, or trying on clothes. I was as confused as any "normal" person would be, and my mind was spinning around. Finally, when it stopped, the first thing I noticed was the disk jockey (D.J).

This D J. was some type of leader who was controlling the crowd with the music he played. Spinning his records first slower and then faster made the crowd almost uncontrollable. He stood laughing as he brought the crowd to the verge of frenzy. His features looked like they had been handpicked by a god of humor and put together in total darkness. His dread locks were of a color that one could get only from a bottle. Pierced ears, nose, lips, and eyebrows gave him a surrealistic appearance. His eyes were as black as nightfall on some cold winter's night, and the clothes he wore were definitely three sizes too big and had a certain appeal of dirt and grime. Obviously, he was not from this planet. Finally, I got enough courage to walk over to the D. J. and ask for Deanne. I had heard of Deanne from friends of mine. They told she was one of the best piercers in Atlanta. The D J. looked at me for a second, smiled, and pointed with his long devilish hand across the store. I turned my head slowly toward where he had pointed, and for an instant, my heart jumped into my throat. My eyes had seen something that they could not yet define. It was as if my mind were flipping through the dictionary, quickly trying to find a definition for the individual. All I could do was nod my head and smile.

I did not expect the tattoos, shaved head, and pierced body of this hideous looking young woman. However, Deanne turned out to be one of the nicest people I met there. I expected her to be lacking in intelligence, but I was wrong. She told me to follow her into the back of the room so that we could get started filling out the paperwork. "So, you want your nipple pierced?" she said. I stood there in complete silence debating what to say. At any moment I was expecting the door to come crashing down and my parents to be on the other side shaking their heads in disgust. "Virgin?" she asked. I responded, "What? I don't think that's any of your . . . ." However, before I could finish my response, she finished by saying, "Your first time, huh?" I turned red as a ripe tomato and said, "Is it that obvious?" She said, "We get all kinds of people in here, and your request is as simple as giving birth to a baby." I wondered if giving birth could be that simple? While I filled out the paperwork, she went over the rules of the establishment. She explained that piercing was not simply about getting pierced; it was a ritual experience, a rite of passage. I finished the paperwork and asked, "Who will be doing the piercing?" "I will," she said. My body went numb for an instant, but I managed to stand tall and strong as I wondered what I had gotten myself into. Deanne then led me over to the shelf where the jewelry was kept and said, "Pick the one that you like." Scanning through the assorted types of accessories, I chose a silver loop with a ball on the end. "All right, I guess you're ready to start the procedure," she said with an evil grin on her face.

The procedure was nothing like I had expected. She led me into a cold, sterile gray room, almost the same kind that one would find in a morgue at a hospital. She told me to take off my shirt and have a seat in the chair. I was sitting when she returned with a tray filled with medical implements. I did not dare ask their purpose, but Deanne noticed the tension in my eyes and immediately started talking. She told me that it wouldn't hurt a bit and that I had nothing to worry about. Within a second, a clamp had been attached to my nipple. I kept hoping that this would be the only pain I would have to endure. The clamp stayed on as she rubbed alcohol all around my nipple. "This has to be one of my favorite parts of the whole procedure," she exclaimed. While she was telling me this, her right hand came up clutching a long menacing needle. "This won't hurt a bit," Deanne said with a gleam in her eyes. I bit my lip as she inserted the long needle into my nipple. Pain was the only thing I could think about, but I endured it for about a minute and thought it wasn't too bad. I thought everything was over, but when I looked down, a needle was sticking through the flesh of my nipple. "How are we doing?" Deanna said. I just nodded my head because my voice had disappeared when the needle took its plunge, and I doubted that it would return anytime soon. Then, she took the ring, sterilized it, and went on to insert it into the hole. What seemed like forever was actually five minutes. "Done," she said, "you can now relax." Deanna then explained that "The pain is gone for now, but when you clean it, it will be sore for a few days." She continued, "Here is a list of products that you need to purchase so your ring won't get infected." I was done.

After the procedure was over, I still had to deal with the aftermath. I got up, put on my clothes, and walked out the door. When I entered the front room again, I saw the D. J. staring in my direction with a smile on his face. I had rebelled against my parents, and I felt good about it. The phoenix had risen from the ashes of my childhood. I left that place knowing that one day I would be back again. However, while I drove home, reality set in. My parents could never find out what I had done. Pandora's Box would have to remain shut, so I kept it hidden for weeks. I felt sneaky because I had never kept anything from my parents. Yet I was old enough to make my own decisions and face the consequences. The guilt had built up inside me so much that I finally broke down and told my mother. She looked at me with vacant eyes and said, "Dear, what in the world are you talking about?" I tried to explain that I had made a mistake and that I was sorry. But before I could finish, she interrupted me and said, "The nipple ring? Honey, I've known about that for weeks." My mouth hit the floor. Am I crazy? At any moment, I expected the men in white suits from the hospital to come in and take me away in a strait jacket. She told me, "You're old enough to make your own decisions. Whatever you choose we'll be proud of you." At that moment, I realized that I had grown up and that my parents were not the little Hitlers that I made them out to be.

◆◆◆

"The limits of my language
mean the limits of my world."

Ludwig Wittgenstein

My Brother's Shadow

Stephanie Richey

English 1101/Narration

My older brother once said, "Your reputation is what you are in the light, and your character is what you are in the dark." During my preteen and early adolescent years, the spotlight of my older and much more successful brother, Doug, had lighted my reputation. Upon my entry to high school, I was left alone in the dark when the two of us, and our identities, were geographically split. During the absence of my best friend and brother, my heart not only grew fonder, but it grew stronger as well.

Throughout the nine years that our family lived in Nashville, Tennessee, I responded to three primary names: Stephanie Richey, Doug Richey's little sister, or lil' Richey. My teachers, youth directors, community leaders, and Doug's peers all knew me because of his reputation and the positive impact he made on them. I quickly learned that such a close connection to him could definitely be used to my benefit. When I introduced myself as Doug Richey's little sister to new teachers or other adults, they would recall his distinguished list of accomplishments and striking personality. They always seemed to expect similar traits and characteristics from the same gene pool. I instantly became one of their favorites. The teachers immediately titled me as "teacher's pet," and youth leaders gave me extra time and attention. Even the cheerleaders at Doug's sporting events would include me because my brother was the hero of Bruin football. Because I was related to a legacy, it seemed as though I was always quickly accepted and rarely had to work for approval.

This constant association with my brother never seemed to be a threat to me until I was forced to lose it. Days after Doug graduated from high school with honors, our family relocated to Atlanta. My brother traveled through the Rockies that summer, and shortly after his return, he left for college. I was left alone in a new city that I did not know and a city that did not know Doug. It seemed as though without big brother's guiding hand, I did not know where to go. I certainly did not think I would survive the crowded halls of Milton High or even the foreign terrain of Alpharetta. My new environment was comprised of roads that my brother had neither traveled nor paved for me. I was driven to develop my own identity in time to start school. I learned to respond only to "Stephanie Richey" and not rely on Doug's fame for recognition. My new teachers and peers knew me by who I was and not by my brother's reputation.

My brother was the first to tell me, "If it does not kill you, it can only make you stronger." Like much of his advice, his voice rang loud and true. With Doug in college, my self-confidence multiplied, and I became much stronger as an individual. Without the consoling hand of my brother, I learned to change struggles into challenges. Learning so quickly about how to build my own reputation and character helped me become a more dedicated worker and devoted leader. I have taken my dedication and applied my leadership to many activities around the school and community. For example, I help out as FCA president, cheerleading captain, Anchor Club committee chair, and section editor of the yearbook. Much of my time is also committed to Young Life and middle school leadership at my church.

As our family watched the home video that my dad filmed of last year's homecoming court, my brother commented on how successful I had been in high school. He was proud of the person I was becoming and thanked me for being an inspiration to him. However, it was Doug who deserved a "thank you" for being such a strong role model for me. He hugged me before he left for school and said, "Lil' Richey, keep growing, keep challenging, keep experiencing, and keep loving." He was then off to his final year of college. No matter how far away Doug goes, I will always hold him close to my heart. His absence and presence will continue to strengthen and challenge me.

Generation Clash

Iman Foufa

ENSL 017/Comparison & Contrast

One of the main reasons why I left my native country of Algeria is that I could not stand people's ideas about life and what was really important. Even though my mom is a somewhat modern person and has some occidental concepts, she still has very strict ideas about what a girl's purpose in life is and what a girl has to do or not do. Although I sometimes agree with my mom's values and beliefs, I completely disagree on two points.

Everyone in this world has a purpose in this life. My mom believes the purpose of a girl's life is to be married. Without marriage, her life is ruined, and there is no happiness. However, my mother did not succeed in her marriage, nor did her sisters or her mother. Moreover, she never liked her conjugal life, but she believes that even though a woman can get the highest degree in academic studies and succeed professionally, she will not be happy and will have no life if she is not married. However, my beliefs are very different from hers; my purpose in this life is to succeed by myself and to succeed first in my studies, then in my professional life, and last in my conjugal life. I believe that a woman can be happy if her other goals are satisfied without being married, but of course, it would be nice if a person is happy combining a professional life and also a conjugal life. However, I understand why my mother has her beliefs. Because the Algerian culture makes women believe that their roles are predetermined, the women think that they don't have a choice or the freedom to choose.

In addition, the Algerian culture is pretty strict about what a girl can do or has to do and what she cannot do or should not do, and my mom has almost the same ideas as the older Algerian generations had. She believes that a girl cannot move from her parents' home to her own place without being married. A "good" girl has to be under her parents' control until she goes under her husband's control, and this is the way it is and nothing else will do. In fact, a girl has no right to decide for herself what is best for her alone nor the right to have her own place for herself and no one with her because the Algerian people care a lot about what "other people think" or what "other people say." Therefore, few women have the courage to move on and to do whatever they want because they will be excluded from society at large and be treated badly. This is why I think my mother has the same ideas; even though she is very liberated, she is afraid of society's opinion. However, I do not have the same values, and I think that since we are in the twentieth century, these kinds of ideas should disappear.

Even though I was raised in Algeria, the country that I love most in this world, and even though I am very proud of my culture, I am very skeptical about some points that my culture leads my mother to believe in. In fact, I think the twentieth century has created equal rights between men and women, and we should be worried about things that are much more important than thinking about what a girl should do or not do.

◆◆◆

"Words are the physicians of
a mind diseased."

Aeschylus

Asmara: Before and After Independence

Habtemariam Gidey

ENSL 017/Comparison & Contrast

Eritrea is a small country on the horn of Africa. It was colonized by Turkey, Italy, Britain, and Ethiopia in that order. The worst of all these periods was the Ethiopian time, which was from 1961 to 1991. Ethiopia had a negative impact on the civilization of Eritrea and on the Eritreans. One can easily realize the worst side of the Ethiopian administration simply by comparing Asmara, the capital city of Eritrea, before and after its independence.

Before the independence of Eritrea, Asmara was like a graveyard waiting to bury its inhabitants. There was no electricity, clean water supply, or means of transportation. People had to travel on foot from one place to another. The roads and bridges were getting older and older, and no one repaired them. There were a limited number of schools, and they were not in proportion to the demand of society's population. Even in these schools, there were no desks for the students nor tables and chairs for the teachers. Nevertheless, countless bars and dance clubs were open all over the city and around the schools. In Asmara, there were more than 500,000 people, but to my surprise, there was only one hospital in the city. At that time, people's movements were also restricted. Everybody had to be at home from 7:00 p.m. to 6:00 a.m.

Right after independence, however, all these conditions changed and improved. Asmarans today enjoy a twenty-four-hour supply of electricity and clean water without limit. The new Eritrean government's economic policies allow investors to participate in public transportation; as a result, more than 100 city buses and about 600 taxis are operating now in Asmara. The government takes the initiative to maintain roads and bridges of the city, and they are in very good condition. The municipality of Asmara banned most of the bars and dance clubs, and those that are still open have a clear code for their operation. For example, anyone under 18 cannot get any service in these bars. If we look at the schools, we see that the ministry of education has provided enough materials to the ones already in existence and has built many new schools to meet the demands of the society. In free Asmara, there is no limit on adults' movements, but children must be at home before 8 p.m. After independence, three hospitals and several clinics were built to meet the health needs of the people.

In 1985, I read an article in Newsweek about Asmara. It said that in 1929, there were only two cities in Africa that had an urban European lifestyle. These were Johannesburg in South Africa and Asmara in Eritrea. From that time until its independence, Asmara did not show any progress while other African cities became relatively developed. Since gaining independence, the government and the people of Asmara have done a lot to solve many of the major problems, but there is still a lot to do in all aspects until Asmara regains its beauty and style.

"The pen is mightier than the sword."

Edward Bulwer-Lytton

Dhahran: Before and After the Gulf War

Katherine Bollan

English 0099/Comparison & Contrast

Dhahran, Saudi Arabia, is my home. I was raised and lived there for eighteen years. In 1991 the Gulf War took place, so there were many American soldiers who came to help us. Many families that didn't want to stay evacuated the kingdom, but my family and I stayed throughout the war. During the war my city changed with the implementation of many safety precautions and restrictions, but after the war, Dhahran became more modernized.

Staying at home during the war was quite an experience. Once the Gulf War began, many American soldiers came to help us save our country. Their presence somewhat changed our way of life. Families that stayed in Dhahran would welcome the soldiers into their homes. We would throw parties and prepare huge meals for them. Basically, we showed them a good time whenever they were able to get away from their stations.

An interesting story occurred one day with a female American soldier. First of all, women cannot drive much in Saudi; we can only drive in our neighborhoods. One female soldier was driving on a highway, and a Saudi man stopped her. He got out of his car and started yelling at her for driving. Holding her gun, she got out of her vehicle and yelled at him, "I'm here saving you and your country, so don't tell me what I can't do." The man got back into his car and drove off without saying anything else. I found that incident funny because she was right for what she said since it was the truth.

Another change was that in our neighborhoods sirens were placed every two blocks. Everybody had gas masks that had to be with us at all times. The kids had curfews of sundown and had to be off of the streets by that time. In school we practiced safety precautions. We had two or three safety drills a week. We could hear the bombs and missiles going off in the distance, and many aircrafts flew overhead every day. One day I was really frightened. The enemy fired a missile about ten miles away from my home. A scud missile was fired from our side to intercept their missile to blow it up in mid-air before it hit anything. The enemy's missile landed in the desert near my neighborhood. The houses shook, and the sirens went off to alert everybody. We had to get in our safety huts, which were either the basement, or if people didn't have a basement, they got into a storage room under the staircase. After the explosions occurred and the sirens stopped wailing, we used to be able to turn on the TV and watch what had happened. Then that had to stop because the enemy would also watch the TV and find out how accurate their missiles were. Once it was safe enough to go out to where the missiles had landed, people would collect pieces of the missiles' debris. Some people made charms out of this debris.

After the war Dhahran became more beautiful with more attractions and greenery. The city changed and became more modernized after the war took place. Green grass and foliage were planted on desert ground. Trees, including palm trees, were also planted. My town began to look more beautiful with all of the lush, green plants. Also, more malls were built downtown. The newest and biggest mall that we have now is three stories tall and mainly has clothes and shoes from Europe. The third level in the mall is a huge food court and an indoor amusement park. In addition, we have fast-food restaurants that we never had before. These restaurants include Taco Bell, Burger King, Popeye's, and Wendy's. New nicer restaurants were built as well. We now have better products and restaurants. Moreover, the war made more people aware of Saudi Arabia, so many families came to Saudi for employment. Obviously, Saudi changed for the better after the end of the war.

Dhahran, Saudi Arabia, is a lovely city with much more to offer than before. Living in a war was an unforgettable experience, but it was an exciting, although terrifying, time for many Saudi residents. All in all, though, positive results came about as a result of the war.

♦♦♦

"Read over your compositions,
and when you meet a passage
which you think is particularly fine,
strike it out."

Samuel Johnson

Atlanta Versus Highlands: Highlands Wins

Lisa Rippon

English 1101/ Comparison & Contrast
(Reprinted from Fourth Edition)

I have lived in a few places in my life, and some have been better than others. I grew up in a small city (35,000 people), lived in an industrial town for a short time, moved to the mountains of western North Carolina, and finally settled here in Atlanta. Although I enjoy living in Atlanta, I find living in Highlands, North Carolina, to be much more peaceful.

One of my main concerns since I've been here in Atlanta is safety. Because of the high crime rate, I don't feel that my property or my person is safe most of the time. I have to make sure my house is locked, my car is locked, and my purse is tucked safely out of reach. Sometimes I think it is too much trouble to go out at all. When I'm with a group of friends, it's not so bad, but even then it's frightening to go out at night. Many times someone asking for money has approached us; my first instinct is to run away. The difference between Atlanta and the Highlands is that in the Highlands I didn't feel scared. People did not have to lock their houses or cars; in fact, when my friends and I would go into town, we would leave our keys in the car. Nighttime was pretty uneventful, so even then I felt safe. I could walk down Main Street by myself, and if someone approached, I'd just say "hello" and walk on by. Sometimes I'd run into someone that I knew, and we'd stop and talk for a few minutes. I felt much more at ease living in Highlands than I do here in Atlanta.

Leisure activities in the two cities (if one can call Highlands a city) are so different that they are hard to compare. Because it is such a big city, Atlanta has a lot of activities to choose from. There are many different types of shopping experiences to be had--from flea markets to Phipps Plaza to Little Five Points.

The one thing they all have in common is that everyone else wants to go there, too! Okay, maybe I'm exaggerating a little bit, but it seems like there is a crowd of noisy, impatient people wherever I go. If I want to do something a bit different, I can always go to the symphony, the museum, or a movie, but again these places are usually crowded. Though Highlands didn't offer such a wide variety of activities, the few activities were usually more relaxed. I would often spend my afternoon breaks taking a short hike in the woods or climbing a nearby waterfall. On the hottest summer days, we would get out of the kitchen for our break, grab the nearest vehicle, and go jump in the river! The water never got above forty-five degrees, but we didn't care. Even at night we'd go swimming after a hard day's work. When special events came up, we'd go to those. Whether it was Oktoberfest at camp, Halloween night in town, or Fourth of July fireworks at Sunset Rock, just about everyone was likely to be there. In a town that had only 2,000 year-round residents, everyone knew almost everyone else, so even if there was a big crowd, I felt more comfortable than I do here in Atlanta because the community was like a family.

Finally, one of the most disparaging differences between the two locations is the scenery. Atlanta has a great skyline for people who like buildings. Personally, I prefer Mother Nature's architecture over that of humans'. At night, the light from the buildings and streetlights makes it seem as bright as day. There are many attractions in the city; some are historical, such as the Cyclorama, some recreational, such as Piedmont Park, and some architectural, such as the older houses in Midtown. People will always be interested in going to see these sights, but the call of the wild is what I like. Where I lived in Highlands, I had a three hundred sixty-degree view right outside my door. The only things to see for miles were mountains, trees, and birds flying high in the sky. I much prefer the smell of earth and trees to the smell of trash and car exhaust. At night, the light show is breathtaking! It never ceases to amaze me how many colors can be seen in one sunset. When the last of the sunlight is fading in the west, the first of the stars come out in the east. On a clear night, it seems as if there is no space between the thousands of stars. It is truly a wondrous sight. If I could choose which to see each night, city lights or a starry sky, I wouldn't hesitate to choose the latter. The stars make me feel at peace with the world.

Although I can choose from a wide spectrum of activities in Atlanta, the atmosphere in Highlands is more laid-back. It is a quiet little community in the mountains where life seems to slow down to a manageable speed and where people say hello when they meet each other. I find Atlanta a fun place to live even though I feel I have to watch my back a lot. If I had a choice (financially speaking), I would have a little cabin in the mountains around Highlands to go to when it gets too noisy for me here in Atlanta. It would be a place where I could relax and enjoy the peace and quiet around me.

◆◆◆

"If you would not be forgotten,
As soon as you are dead and rotten,
Either write things worthy reading,
Or do things worth the writing."

Benjamin Franklin

What Skateboarding Means to Me

Andrew Gilley

English 0098/Cause & Effect

When I reflect on my life, there are not too many things that I can say that I have fun doing. My life consists of going to work, leaving work, and going to school. I do not experience times that remind me of what being a child was like. One day I actually took the time to think about what I could do to bring myself back to that carefree lifestyle. This was when I decided to ride my skateboard again. I had not ridden a skateboard since I was six years old, but I could not let this stop my search for the good old days. I enjoy skateboarding because it is something that brings me a great deal of satisfaction, offers a sense of daring, and helps me to forget about my dull, everyday life.

Skateboarding has brought so much to me. One of the things it has given me is a sense of satisfaction and accomplishment. I will work on a trick for days at a time, sometimes even weeks. Once, I even worked on one trick for six months. I would go out to the front of my house for hours at a time, trying to land a footwrap (when the skateboarders spin the skateboard three hundred-sixty degrees around their foot while riding forward). I finally landed it one day, and a great sense of accomplishment came over me. This feeling is one that cannot be put into words. With just going to work and school all of the time, I had lost the feeling of reaching a goal. I am the type of person who needs to feel that I have reached a different goal every day.

Another sense of enjoyment I find in skateboarding is the daring factor. When I am looking at a fifteen-foot long handrail, a sense of nervousness comes over me. The scared feeling that I get right before I try a difficult trick gives me an adrenaline rush.

This is what makes me want to do it more. If I actually take the time to think about the consequences, I will never attempt the trick. This scared feeling makes the trick all the more satisfying when it is over.

The most important reason why I skateboard is that it helps me to lose touch with reality. From the minute that I walk into the skate park until the time that I leave, I have no thoughts on my mind, so my mind takes a break from the realities of life. I don't think about how broke I am, nor do I think about the big test that I have coming up; I just enjoy life. These feelings of joy and happiness overcome all of my problems and remind me of what being a twelve-year-old was like.

Skateboarding brings me many different feelings, but most importantly, it has brought satisfaction, enjoyment, and escape into my life. In a sense, it is my own meditation because it relaxes me in a way that nothing else can. Maybe if everyone found a hobby he or she loves as much as I love skateboarding, the world would be a more relaxed place to live.

◆◆◆

"There is but one art,
to omit."

Robert Louis Stevenson

Combining School and Work

Amber Walschleger

English 0098/Cause & Effect

I am one of the many students forced to work while I attend college. It is the only choice that I have if I want to be successful. Many others are lucky; they have other sources to support them and to pay for their schooling. However, I know that I am not alone in my category either. I am taking night classes with many other students, and they have given me support by sharing some of their solutions to the problem of combining work and school. Some of the difficulties I have combining school and work are managing time, handling stress, and staying focused.

The first problem that I encountered when I started school was managing my time. I had been accustomed to free time after work. I would come home from work and be grateful that my day was over. Now, I never have that luxury. I have two jobs. One job is to support my household and myself. The other is to pay for my schooling and books. I work Monday to Friday from 8:00 a.m. to 5:00 p.m. at my first job, and I have Monday and Wednesday classes from 5:30 p.m. to 10:00 p.m. By the time that I get home, it's straight to bed for me. Tuesdays are the days that I am slammed with homework. Thursdays are my days to catch up. I know that I have four days to schedule my duties and homework at a pace that I can handle. I usually work out on Thursdays. I think that it is good to keep one relaxing activity for myself. Friday is my day to make up for what I didn't do on Thursday. Then, I work at my second job from 11:00 a.m. to 8:00 p.m. on Saturdays and every other Sunday. I look forward to my two days off even though I always end up sleeping.

The second problem that I have combining work and school is handling stress. My job has many stresses that I deal with on a daily basis. I have to make sure that I am doing my job correctly, keeping track of my co-workers, and maintaining a positive attitude throughout the day. The stress from school is different. I worry about my grades, deadlines for homework, and understanding all of the information for which I am responsible. Then to add to it, I have to deal with the different social atmospheres at school and at work. I think that I handle stress in positive ways. I like to workout at least twice a week, and I take short breaks throughout the day to focus on my priorities.

The hardest challenge that I face is staying focused. At the beginning of the quarter, I start with a positive attitude. My mind is focused on school. I have plans to work hard daily so that I can achieve the grades that I am striving for. Then, as the semester goes by, I get burned out because there seems to be no end to the schoolwork, and it seems that I have no time for myself. I am worn down with no motivation. I begin to notice that I am not getting my work done and that my grades are falling. This is when my motivation kicks back in. I think about all of the money that I have spent and the time and effort that I have already put in. I then decide that I am not going to let myself fail, so I get back into my usual routine and work hard once again.

There are many obstacles that I overcome so that I can go to school because it gives me a feeling of satisfaction knowing that I am trying to better myself. I know that this is what I need to do in order to be successful. My hard work and dedication will be recognized once I receive my degree. Then when I come home from work, I will really appreciate being able to come home and relax for a couple of hours.

◆◆◆

The Benefits of Participating In Sports

Cecilia LaBar

English 0099/Cause & Effect

Many children participate in various types of sports. They usually get started with a couple of sports at one time; for example, some play baseball in the summer, football in the winter, and basketball in the spring. Though they may play these sports all year long, they will usually stick with one certain sport from their childhood years through their teens. Some benefits from playing such sports are learning valuable social skills, gaining confidence and self-esteem, and competing in a positive way.

When playing sports, children interact with people of the same age and grade. They will learn many valuable social skills through sports. It is important for children to communicate with each other. Once the communication begins between fellow athletes, they are able to state their opinions on what plays could have or should have happened during certain times of the game. A child's ability to voice his or her opinion and make statements is very important. He or she will not only be able to speak out on sports but also in the classroom and in the future as well. When a child plays a sport for a long period of time with the same people, he or she gets to know the teammates as well as the sport.

While the social skills of children playing sports are improved, winning is also a positive experience because it boosts their self-esteem and confidence level. For example, the result of the game may depend on a little boy at bat in a baseball game. He swings at two in a row, and then BAM, the batter hits the runners home. The fate of the game depended on this one child, and he won the game for the team. This player gets the game ball and is considered the M.V.P. That child wasn't sure what was going to happen in that game, but as it turns out, everyone thinks of him as a hero. Now that child has a feeling that he can do anything. When children feel like that, it makes them determined to play better. These are important factors when growing up. A child could be just as determined to make good grades and get into a good college. Confidence is a major factor that helps children successfully get through the years to come.

Confidence is a trait that everyone needs, and so is the ability to compete with others in a positive way. When playing on a sports team, a person should be able to learn the fundamentals of being competitive. The teams will play other teams and learn that when losing, they must exhibit good sportsmanship. A person participating in sports will learn this skill and be able to use it in the future. Learning to be competitive will be necessary in school and in many jobs. A school play is one example of a competitive situation. After auditions, a child looks at the cut list and sees that his or her name is cut from the play. His or her game theory is to keep trying and to do better next time. In a company, there might be a promotion spot open, and several employees might be up for it. Everyone is trying really hard, but an outsider gets the job. People who have the confidence and good sportsmanship will not complain, and they will keep working and believing that they can somehow get noticed at another time. By being an athlete, a person will learn to compete in a positive way.

Athletes can learn so much from playing sports, such as being sociable, gaining confidence, and competing positively. A person should be able to socialize with other people, make lots of friends, and gain confidence. Competitiveness is also crucial in the business world. All of these skills can be learned from participating in sports.

♦♦♦

The Lack of Communication in Families

Jill Huang

English 1101/Cause & Effect

According to a recent study, a teen talks to his/her parents for approximately ten minutes a day; of this ten minutes, five are usually spent arguing. What causes such bad communication between children and their parents? The reason is simple, but it is often overlooked: our busy lifestyles do not allow us to spend enough quality time with our families because of rushed mornings, nonexistent family dinners, and preoccupied weekends.

A Friday night sitcom portrays the typical rush-and-go morning of a family. In one episode, the mother cheerfully prepares breakfast for her family. Suddenly, the father rushes down the stairway, gives her a quick peck on the cheek, then heads out the door. Next comes her son. "Would you like to have some breakfast this morning, Corrie?" his mother earnestly asks. "Sorry mom. I gotta run. See ya." And he is gone. Finally, the disappointed mother pleads for her daughter to stay for breakfast. However, anxious to catch her bus on time, she also prepares to leave. Just as the breakfast turns cold, so does the poor mother's heart. Many families replay this scene every morning. Because the family members do not have time to eat, they also neglect any peaceful familial conversations.

Another reason for this lack of communication is the decline of supper time enjoyed by the entire family. This shared experience should be the perfect time for them to talk about their days. I have noticed that many families do not even eat suppers together because of sports practices, part-time jobs, or maybe even conflicting class schedules. They can no longer benefit from this valuable time of listening and sharing; in turn, this lack of time together impacts upon the cohesiveness of families.

Not only are we busy during weekdays, but our time is also often occupied over the weekends. When are we supposed to spend some family time together? Dad may have to work extra hours on weekends to supplement family income, mom busies herself with all kinds of cleaning and cooking, and children will probably spend the whole day with their friends. Our weekends provide yet another denial of family time.

As families spend less time together, the generation gap deepens even further. Already we can hardly understand each other's beliefs and motives. Due to this lack of communication, we now feel little more respect for family members than we do for strangers. In my family, I do not see my parents very often during the week. When we do sit down for dinner, we watch TV instead of talking to each other. After dinner, my parents will read their newspapers, and I have to study. Whenever we talk, we always have very little patience with each other. We are so preoccupied with other things that we have neglected one of the most important values--family bonding.

Now my family has unofficially designated a time to take walks together every night. Through this bonding time, I can express my opinions and feelings to my parents and also learn more about their perspectives on things. Working on communication skills takes time and commitments from both parents and children. More importantly, this relationship can be one of our most rewarding accomplishments; therefore, it is well worth all the work.

The Animal That Makes the Worst Apartment Pet

Pamela Hopkins

English 0098/ Analysis

I live in a three-bedroom apartment on the third floor. The apartments are really nice, and they are in a nice area. There is just one problem--they are over-run with dogs. It would not be so bad if there were one or two here or there. However, in my complex sometimes it seems as if there are more dogs than tenants. They are not cute, little cuddly house pets. A lot of them are as big as horses. The three aspects that I hate the most about having so many dogs around are the loud barking, horrible odor, and the terror of being chased by these dogs.

Barking dogs are some of my worst enemies. They bark as long and as loud as they possibly can. The dogs in my complex seem to bark in sequence and harmony. The high-pitched barks usually start during the early morning hours. The medium tone barkers usually wait until lunchtime. Finally, the bass tone barkers take over after dark and carry on until it is time to change shifts again. The more that I scream and yell at them, the louder they bark. I used to think that dogs were like babies and would bark only if they were hungry, sick, or wanted attention, but not the dogs in my complex. Sometimes I think that they compete to see which one can bark the loudest and longest. I find myself dreaming about barking because I hear it so much. Because I live in an apartment complex that allows dogs, I certainly do not need an alarm clock.

What I do need is something to kill the horrible odor. Unlike the barking, I really only have to deal with the odor when I am coming from or going to my apartment. As long as I am inside my apartment, my nose is safe. Outside of my apartment sometimes the odor is so bad that I literally have to inhale and hold my breath until I am safely inside of my car before I exhale. I do not know if my neighbors believe in grooming their pets or not, but it smells as if they bathe the dogs in horse manure. When it rains, that just adds to the terrifying smell. If I wanted to endure a scent as horrible as a stinking, wet, smelly dog, then I would relocate to a farm.

Sometimes I think that I would rather live on a farm than be chased by some of the dogs in my complex. Some of these dogs are really big. There are some that are as tall as my waistline. When a dog chases someone, it is for one or two reasons. In my opinion, they are either playing, or they want some human meat. I really do not care to have to determine the difference. I do not like playing with dogs, especially really big ones. Therefore, I am going to think that they are chasing me for one reason and one reason only; they want to have me for dinner. I have learned one thing about being chased by a dog, though. I should not run unless it runs after me first. But if it does run after me first, I am ready to run and run very fast.

I know that some dogs out there are man's best friend, and I have to admit that, in general, I do like dogs. However, small dogs that are quiet are my favorite. As a matter of fact, as a child, I owned several dogs. But at that time I did not live in an apartment. And now that I do, I would never own a dog, and I think they should be banned from living in apartments. So for all of the dog owners that are living in an apartment, I have one suggestion for them—they should get a bird as a pet.

"The waste basket is a writer's best friend."

Isaac Bashevis Singer

The Good Boss

Jean C. Trent

English 0099/Analysis

The good or bad qualities of a boss affect how employees perform on the job. There are many characteristics that help a good boss communicate effectively, skillfully, and tactfully with his/her employees. The three qualities that make for a good boss are patience, a positive attitude, and understanding.

The first quality that makes a good boss is patience. Patience is a necessary ingredient that he/she must possess in order to conquer important tasks. Newcomers to the business may provide a challenge for the boss, for he/she must teach them what their priorities and responsibilities consist of. The good boss knows that in order to teach or demonstrate effectively, he must not use rash words or actions, for the employees may not follow the boss' instructions clearly. Therefore, the good boss chooses to be observant, quiet, and tactful. Patience can lead to successful business and can create a healthy future for the company. As Ralph Waldo Emerson once advised, "Adopt the pace of nature: her secret is patience."

The second factor that a good boss has is a positive attitude. The goodness that shines in the boss will reflect onto the staff members and create a positive, rejuvenating, and comfortable atmosphere. The boss holds the "keys to success" for the company because he/she is the main role model. Furthermore, customers and employees alike enjoy interacting with one another when the environment feels safe and comfortable. The lack of a positive role model could lead to a state of either dissatisfaction or discontent. Thus, many people find it easier to recall a negative experience with a company than a positive experience. Therefore, the business can depend on the good or bad attitude of the management or the employees. The optimism of a good boss will spread throughout the company.

The final characteristic that is common to a good boss is understanding. Understanding employees and customers can be difficult, especially in the midst of confusion from interrupting phone calls and paperwork. When a good boss takes time out to talk with employees about personal or job-related issues, the employee gains respect and admiration for the boss. Through the understanding eyes of the boss, the employee feels reassured and confident in his/her progress with the company. Communicating with the employees helps solve problems and creates open doors for any other concerns that they might have.

Therefore, the three qualities that create a good boss are patience, positive attitude, and understanding. Authority figures in a business environment can bring either strengths or weaknesses to the work environment. However, having these necessary characteristics makes any boss a good one.

"I like good strong words that mean something."

Louisa May Alcott

My Bed

Kathy Thompson

English 1101/Analysis

A bed in and of itself is just a bed. It is merely pieces of wood and metal constructed with just enough spacing in between to fit a mattress snug within its borders. My vision of a bed goes much further than that. My favorite place on earth happens to be my bed. Memories of my childhood, reminders of my family's past, and hopes for current times all encompass the love of my bed. My bed and the function of my bed play an important role in my life.

As a child, my parents' bed was a place of security and comfort. Long, stormy nights were often spent beside my parents in the comfort of their bed. An illness or a bad day also meant a stay in their bed. Of course, it could have been my parents that emitted the comfort, but I was definitely soothed by being in the mammoth-sized bed and feeling swallowed by mountains of sheets and blankets. My own childhood bed had its special moments as well: endless pillow fights with friends and cousins, secretly hiding under the bed during a game of hide-and-go-seek, and using my bed as a trampoline while living out my childhood dream of being a gymnast. As a teenager, all of life's trivial problems were solved on endless telephone conversations while stretched out on my bed. Tears were spilled, laughter was bellowed, and homework was agonized over all in the comfort of my bed.

The attributes of my current bed provide a tie to my family's past. The headboard and footboard, constructed in the early 1900's, were once owned by my husband's grandparents. The headboard, grandiose at first sight, has intricately carved stalks of wheat embedded in the center while scalloped edges adorn the top and sides. Many untold stories and secrets are buried deep into the grains of that dark amber mahogany. A soft, tattered quilt with red, blue, and green gingham squares gently covers the bed's mattress. This quilt made so daintily and painstakingly by the hands of my Great Aunt Esmer is one of my favorite family heirlooms. Soft, fluffy goose-down pillows piled high upon the bed were given to my husband and me as a wedding gift from my grandparents.

My bed serves as more than just a place to lay my head after a long, weary day. Dreams are dreamt, plans are made, late night talks conspire, love is made, books are read, food is eaten, naps are taken, and favorite episodes of *The Wonder Years* are watched. More than just a bed, it serves as my home base. It is a place that I know will always be there for me, a place that I know I can always go to hide away from the world and be in peace, and a place that I long for on days when I am not feeling well, on days that are cold and stormy, and on days that nothing seems to be going my way. No matter where I go or how far I travel, the same words are always uttered from my mouth, "I cannot wait to sleep in my own bed!"

The English poet Thomas Hood describes the bed as "That heaven upon earth to the weary head." I describe it as a place of serenity, a place that cries out for me every night, and a place that holds its grip on me every morning, begging to embrace me for just one more hour. At first glance, a bed really is just a bed; however, deep within that glance a bed is so much more than just a place to sleep. It is a place to dream and to energize my soul. My bed means more to me than any other place on earth because when I am sleeping in my bed, I know that I am in my own world and at home with my family.

◆ ◆ ◆

Sex Sells

Melissa Watkins

English 1101/Analysis

Oh, what a glorious thing to be young and beautiful! A perfect body, the waft of a beautiful scent, and a flawless complexion are the aim of America's women. At least, advertisers seem to think so. Most modern advertisements portray women as one-dimensional. Ads are made to lure a consumer into purchasing that product, and advertisers will go to any length to achieve this goal. The purpose of advertisement is to leave the consumer with the idea of "if only." The industries of clothing, fragrance, and beauty products exemplify the manipulative sex appeal used in advertising.

The clothing industry is notorious for its shapely or shapeless (whichever the case may be) models that pose ideally for the world to see. Names like Versace and Lazar are renowned for their ever-so-thin models draped in stylish clothes that expose just enough flesh. Versace, for example, has an ad with five different full-length pictures of a woman who, in two of the pictures, is displaying jackets. These pictures blatantly reveal her breasts and what she isn't wearing underneath. Lazar's ad doesn't even show the model's face, just her body with her chest toppling out of a constrictive dress. This particular strategy used by the advertiser objectifies the model; she is no longer a person but a sex symbol. Though clothing is essential to the body, is the barrage of sex necessary to sell the clothes?

An advertisement for fragrance also revolves around a woman's desirability. For advertisers to sell a product they must feature the ideal image, and that image should exemplify what a person wants to feel or look like if he or she wears that scent. Calvin Klein's Kate Moss is a prime example of this "ideal image. "*Vogue* magazine's October '97 issue has Moss captured in a black and white photo with a tube top revealing her midriff. With her arms wrapped tightly around her breasts, the ad simply states, "Be hot. Be cool. Just be." She is statuesque, expressionless except for an almost seductive stare. The ad makes the onlooker yearn to look as "cool" as Moss appears.

On the other hand, Aveda fragrance advertises not with a scantily clad, anorexic model, but with words and pictures of its product. This seems innocent, right? Well, with innuendoes like "touch yourself" and "practice safe scents," this so-called "innocent" picture insinuates sex. Another fragrance that uses sex appeal is Navy with its featured model in a tight dress, long legs, and, of course, the ubiquitous man at her side. What woman wishes she didn't look like these models? Amazingly enough, some women allow themselves to be manipulated into thinking they will walk away just as sexy if they use these fragrances.

Along with clothing and fragrance, beauty products play into the ploy of "wear our makeup and you'll be flawless." There are no Maybelline models that have huge pimples on the end of their noses. On the contrary, the complexion is smooth, the skin wrinkle-free, and the makeup perfect. Estee Lauder's model for foundation is an elegant woman possessing a slender frame, dark eyes, and an almost naive smile. The actual words used in the advertisement include flawless, smooth, and impeccable. Foundation adds color to a person's face, right? The advertisement is set in black and white, preventing the consumer from seeing the foundation's color. Once again, the consumer is led to believe she can be as sexy and young looking as the model displayed.

Although women look with envy, and sometimes hope, to the advertisements of today, are they likely to achieve the perfection they're looking at? Advertisers are clever when they display Kate Moss sitting in her underwear when the ad is for socks. Is the public aware of this ploy? The manipulation is subtle but, nonetheless, there. A woman is not one-dimensional. She doesn't have to be attired in Versace with her hair slicked back, wearing Navy, and conveying arrogance. However, because sex is prominent in everyday life, sex sells.

◆◆◆

"Art thou a pen, whose task shall be
To drown in ink
What writers think?
Oh, wisely write,
That pages white
Be not the worse for ink and thee."

Ethel Lynn Beers

How To Catch A Trout

Dino Tufekcic

ENSL 017/Process Analysis

Most people have gone fishing at least once in their lives. All of them hoped to go back home with a trophy trout, but most went back home empty-handed because they thought that their expensive equipment was the only thing necessary to catch a rainbow trout. The rainbow trout is a smart fish, and in order to catch it, you need a lot of knowledge, patience, and proficiency.

First, in order to catch a rainbow trout, you have to know where to look for it, what it eats, and what equipment to use. The rainbow trout lives in clear, fast mountain streams. It loves rivers with a lot of turns and rocks. You should not look for it in huge, slow, dirty waters because this is not a trout's habitat. Also, in order to be a successful trout fisherman, you should know that the trout feeds on smaller fish, flies, and worms. Therefore, flies are the best bait for big trout, and they are also the most fun. Worms and lizards are good bait as well, but you will not fool a grown trout with this bait. Another thing you have to know to be a good fisherman is how to prepare your equipment. You should never use huge hooks because even the biggest trout do not have large mouths. In addition, you must know how to tie your hooks on the main string so that you do not lose your dinner.

The next thing you have to know is that every good fisherman must be patient while fishing. If you do not love nature, you will never be a successful fisherman. Sometimes it takes very long to catch anything. If this happens to you, it probably means that you have not chosen the best place for fishing or that you are too loud, so the fish is too scared to come closer to you. You should always try to hide yourself as much as possible to be successful.

Proficiency is also a very important part of fishing, especially in fishing for the rainbow trout. A lot of people do not catch anything because they are not skilled enough in reacting and fighting the fish. Once you feel the trout has taken your bait, you must react fast. If you are fast enough, the trout will be on the end of your string, but the challenge is not over yet. You must know how to bring the trout towards you and how to pull it out. Most people, after the trout takes the bait, start pulling it towards the shore with all of their strength, thinking they have caught their dinner. Some of them get the fish to their tables, but most of them lose it. To be certain you catch the trout, you have to fight it. You must let it go its way for a while and slowly pull the string towards you. After you have gotten the fish close to shore, you should try to get its head above the water for a second. This trick makes the fish lose its breath and makes it weak. This advantage helps you bring it to the shore and pull it out. Fishing this way is more fun than just dragging the fish to the shore.

If you follow these steps and if you love nature as much as I do, you will become a good fisherman. If you do not like these steps, you will probably continue to go back home empty-handed, thinking about the trout that slipped through your hands; I, however, will keep having trout for dinner every time I go fishing.

♦♦♦

"This morning I took out a comma, and this afternoon I put it back again."

Oscar Wilde

Late Night Snack

David Marshall

English 1101/Process Analysis

Eating has always been a favorite pastime of mine. Coming from an Italian family, food has been a central point of my life. Every family gathering has revolved around eating. It's no wonder I grew up with another favorite pastime which was cooking. I learned a lot from my mother, watching and waiting in the kitchen for the heavenly smell to come out of the oven and onto my plate. As I grew older, she would let me help and later allowed me free reign of the kitchen. I was frying, boiling, and baking. The hardest part was cleaning up the hurricane-like messes I made. Nevertheless, cooking has always been fun. Even more fun was the enjoyable task of eating my creations. One of my favorites is yellow cake with chocolate frosting. This effortless, satisfying creation has been my favorite nighttime snack although my scale would wish it wasn't.

My adventure starts with a trip to the grocery store. I grab a basket, and I'm off on my trek. I wander past the produce and weave through the canned vegetables. Finally, turning a corner, I feast my eyes on any dessert lovers' delight--the cake and cookie section. I stand in awe of the many selections. Tempted as I am to reach for anything chocolate, I know my late-night craving will find satisfaction in one thing alone: yellow cake with chocolate frosting. As a side note, I'm also a frugal shopper. I search for the least expensive, name brand cake and frosting. I dash through the remainder of my grocery list, and I'm off to the checkout counter. Driving home, my stomach growls in anticipation of the delectable dessert. Arriving home, I check my phone messages and head toward my favorite room in the house, the kitchen. Stowing the lesser important groceries for future preparation, I eye the box cake and its short sidekick. I quickly lose an argument with myself about the alternative of going to the gym so that my pants fit better and prepare to create my late-night snack.

Fighting my male instinct to rush head first into making the concoction, I glance over the instructions. Three eggs, one and one third cup of water, and one-quarter cup of cooking oil are all I need. I open the refrigerator and a cabinet door and bring out all of the ingredients. Next, I grab a bowl and baking pan out of the cupboard to prepare the mixture. I follow the first instructions and pre-heat the oven to 350 degrees. I use spray grease instead of shortening and flour. Simplicity and efficiency are key words to my style of cooking. I mix the ingredients in a large bowl and pour the batter into the greased pan, carefully leaving a small amount of batter as a sample of things to come. The pan goes into the oven. Then the test comes; am I able to bear the thirty-five minute wait? Trying to preoccupy myself, I set the timer. An eternity passes. Then to my delight the buzzers sing its song of rejoicing. I carefully remove the nearly finished product from the oven.

One hour until bedtime, and I slowly think over the hectic day of school and work. Remembering the things on my "to do" list and mentally discarding the items I've accomplished, I allow the cake its cool-down time. Finally, a voice of reason enters my head. I decide not to frost the cake as appeasement to the gods of the scale and have plain cake and one percent milk As I end my day, I find complete satisfaction in this simple treat. Once again, my enjoyment of cooking results in the more enjoyable task of eating.

“The writer must write what he has to say, not speak it.”

Ernest Hemingway

Coffeehouses

Deborah Goldman

English 0099/Classification

Coffee has been around for ages, but today all over the country there is an explosion of gourmet coffeehouses. These coffeehouses are places to sit and ponder. The atmosphere is very casual, and I always feel safe and comfortable inside. Besides the atmosphere, what makes a coffeehouse successful? I think it's the combination of the espressos, lattes, and cappuccinos.

A night out for me is a visit to my local coffeehouse. As I enter the glass doors, I am engulfed by the warm aroma of coffee and the sound of people talking. I make my usual purchase of a tall skinny vanilla latte. Walking through the room with my latte in hand, I notice the usual assortment of customers. Somehow they all seem to mingle here comfortably.

First of all, the espresso customers arrive at a decent hour. They are the local residents who frequent the coffeehouse regularly. They like their coffee dark and extremely strong. No steamed milk or flavoring is added. A straight espresso is made with dark roasted coffee beans and water. The espresso customers are well-dressed older men and women. I think of them as the "master" coffee drinkers.

Equally important to the success of a coffeehouse is the latte customer. The latte drinkers are the families of a coffeehouse. They arrive with children in hand. The families are greeted with friendly service and made to feel welcome. The children sit in big, comfy chairs and play games of checkers or Scrabble. The coffeehouse also has a special selection of drinks for just for kids. The drinks come with silly monsters that are finger puppets. The latte crowd brings joy and laughter to the whole room. It reminds me of sitting around the kitchen table playing cards with my family. However, when there are several big groups of children, they can get a little wild. Soon these kids are back under control by parents who have had enough for one night. With their departure, another important customer arrives.

Finally, the "infants" of coffee drinkers come in. They are the cappuccino drinkers. The cappuccino drinkers are college students who are dying to break away from the tedious restrictions imposed by their parents. I can see this attitude in the way they dress. It's not uncommon to see orange hair and pierced eyebrows. They are the smokers of the coffeehouse and, for this reason, tend to hang around outside. They love their cappuccinos in various flavors and can drink them hot or cold.

All in all, I'm not sure which of these groups I fit into, but anyone who frequents a coffeehouse will hopefully experience the excitement of the different people. The concept of the gourmet coffeehouse is relatively new, but if there's a good combination of different people, it can be a success.

◆◆◆

"True ease in writing comes from art, not chance."

Alexander Pope

Alert or Ignorant?

Carrie Collins

English 1101/ Argument

Excited butterflies flitted around my stomach as I prepared my horse Fritz to go into the show arena. I secured the straps of his protective leg gear for the "umpteenth" time and readjusted the cheek piece of his bridle to make sure it was comfortable for him. He nuzzled my arm affectionately, and I planted a big kiss on his forehead in return. With a last tug on a misbehaving braid, I stood back and admired my sleek and polished horse realizing with a rueful grin that, once again, he looked cleaner and much neater than I. With that, I swung easily up into the saddle and immediately felt his body surge with excitement. Fritz knew exactly why he was here, and he loved every minute of it. I rode up to the arena where a jumping class should have taken place, but in its stead was an animal rights protest in progress. Holding big whips, the protesters blocked the entrance to the arena denying entry to all riders and horses. The basis of their protest was that horses used in competition are abused, resulting in malnutrition, overwork, and serious leg damage. Although some people feel that it is abusive to use horses in competition, they are ignorant of the individualized programs of nutrition, exercise, and leg care that most show horses receive.

Animal rights protesters became alert to the miserable conditions to which the show horses were subjected in the 1992 Barcelona Olympic Games. The oppressive heat, lack of water, and dangerous, unyielding courses proved to be disastrous conditions for both horses and riders. American equestrians, as well as animal rights organizations, immediately became alarmed. It was soon after this event that the animal rights people began to protest against showing horses here in the U.S. They complained that animals didn't receive proper nutrition and were cruelly overworked. They also stated that jumping caused extreme stress to the horses' legs and that it could easily result in injury. These issues were taken to court in Georgia in June of 1995 in hopes of banning all horse competition, including the 1996 Equestrian Olympics. The Animal Rights Organization lost their suit to the vehement and victorious opposition of the horse owners, but they have continued the battle to make their voices heard regarding their "pet issues."

The first of these issues is that animal rights protesters contend that show horses are not given the adequate amounts or types of food they need. On the contrary, these equines benefit from elite and personalized menus. Each horse receives a prescribed amount and specified type of grain tailored to its individual needs according to size, temperament, exercise schedule, and event demands. In fact, served twice daily, the grain portions affect a horse like a high protein energy bar affects an athlete. In addition to this, the provisions of grass, fresh hay, water, and special supplements help to promote a shiny coat and strong hooves. In light of these facts, the animal rights protesters might have a more valid complaint regarding spoiling the show horses rather than abusing them.

Another inaccurate assumption of the animal rights protesters is that show horses are overworked. This is not true. Training show horses is a slow and carefully graduated process. The horses first start out with small exercises and then gradually and methodically build up to the levels of strength and agility necessary to compete. Like any sport, hours of daily practice are required to move up through each level of expertise essential for competition. Tailored workouts are as healthy for the horses' lungs and heart as individualized exercise is for humans. In fact, show horses in upper-level competitions, such as the Olympics, have their own personal veterinary trainers much like the sports trainers for the riders. As a result, show horses are exceptionally well-trained, but not overworked.

Coupled with the contentions regarding nutrition and

overwork is the animal rights protesters' concern regarding leg injuries. They should be aware that a prime concern to all equestrians is the meticulous care of the legs of their horses. It is a proven fact that competing, especially jumping, can stress the horses' legs. However, owners and riders use extreme caution in this area of critically needed protection and care. The horses' legs are either protected by splint or bell boots, which shield the tendons and hooves, or they are polo wrapped in long, wool bandages to prevent pulled or strained muscles. After exercising, training, or eventing, the horses receive a liniment massage. The owners or trainers become personal masseuses and directly apply the liniment, rubbing it all over the horses' legs and massaging the muscles. An athletic trainer does much the same thing in giving a rub down to an athlete after practice. While possible leg injury is a concern to both the animal rights protesters and horse owners, equestrians have long ago given critical attention to extensive prevention of injury in this area.

Since 1995, equestrians have mandated newer, more rigid rules complemented by stricter inspections for all equestrian competitions. These changes were made to eliminate the conditions that can lead to abuse and injury to horses during competition. Therefore, equestrians who wish to compete here in the U.S. must establish and maintain intricate and individualized programs in which the horses receive the utmost attention in nutrition, exercise, and leg care. The animal rights protesters should definitely be alert, but they should certainly not remain ignorant.

◆◆◆

"A single word often betrays a great design."

Jean Baptiste Racine

Classic Television Needs To Make A Comeback

Katie Lowder

English 1101/Argument

With the development of cable, more families are choosing to stay at home and use their television sets as a form of entertainment. But the networks inundate television today with violence, sex, and other explicit topics. It is very difficult to find a show that will amuse the whole family in a good, clean fashion. To reestablish a more pleasurable form of family entertainment, television shows of yesteryear need to make a comeback because of ethical programming, wholesome story lines, and the absence of violence and sex.

Television of yesteryear produced ethical programming that was enjoyable for the whole family. One type of programming was the family shows which portrayed nuclear and non-nuclear family units in a positive light. On Leave It To Beaver, the Beaver could count on his mother's being home and available for any problem he needed to discuss with her. We could also count on his dad providing for the welfare of the whole family. On The Andy Griffith Show, Opie knew that Aunt Bea would be there to take care of him while his dad worked as the town's sheriff. Both programs portrayed middle-class America as having productive and upstanding family members. Most included in the programming were wholesome comedy shows and mystery shows. The comedy shows dealt with humor in a clean, slap-stick manner using nonaggressive issues. On I Love Lucy, Lucy always got the laugh by poking fun at herself or involving herself in humorous circumstances. For example, Lucy got a job working in a candy factory wrapping pieces of candy. The conveyor belt was moving faster than Lucy could wrap the candy, so she started stuffing her mouth with the candy! This scene was very funny without being aggressive or abusive. The mystery shows dealt with the facts not the violence. By using strictly deductive reasoning and interrogation tactics, Perry Mason would find the murderer in a nonviolent and intelligent way.

Furthermore, such classic television shows dealt with wholesome story lines. These programs showed the family interacting with each other. On the Leave It To Beaver show or Father Knows Best show, the family always sat at the dinner table and discussed what had happened in their lives for that day. There were no outside distractions such as the television or radio. Opie and his father, Andy, were always spending quality time together fishing, going on a picnic, or just sitting on the front porch talking. The portrayal of open communication among family members and the respecting of each other's feelings is a novel ideal in the present. Negative influences in their every day life - issues they "created" for a show's topic - were dealt with in a rational manner. No one yelled or lost their temper. Andy would send Opie to his room when he, Opie, got into trouble. Andy would calm down, gather his thoughts and then go upstairs to talk to his son about what happened. The Beaver would also be sent to his room while Ward and June decided what should be done. Each "created incident" dealt with the teaching of a lesson. Opie, for instance, learned that when a person lies it can lead to more lies and hurt the people the lies affected. He was shown that there are consequences and that he must accept the responsibility for his actions. Opie had to tell everyone directly involved that he had lied, apologize, and do what was necessary to correct any problems that resulted from his lies.

Most importantly, television programs of old steered away from violence and sex. On Perry Mason, the victim's feet were shown, his body lying on the floor. The absence of slash scenes and blood and gore still netted the same result: someone was dead. However, the act of how he got that way was left up to the viewer's imagination. When a show dealt with a violent issue the matter was an occurrence that feasibly would happen to an average person or family. For instance, children dealt with the neighborhood bully rather than the neighborhood bully shooting everyone on the playground. Moreover, someone getting hurt falling out of tree instead of being in intensive care because of a car chase kept disaster at a distance. On a different note, but equally important, sex was not dominant in old television shows. The sexual act was implied discreetly with the couple holding hands and walking into the bedroom. Lucy and her husband, Ricky, slept in separate beds, yet Lucy still became pregnant one season. If a television show were so bold as to show a couple kissing, the camera would fade to black before anything else physical took place. Also, in another area of sexual connotation, the manner of dress reflected class and style; it did not promote sex or sleaze. On the whole the costumes used in older television were flattering but not form-fitting. The females had respectable hem lengths of below the knee for their dresses and right at the knee for their shorts. Men wore suits and ties, even to dinner at home. If anyone chose to be casual and have their shirt open, it only involved the top two buttons being undone. And no one ever went around in any state of undress or nudity. Marge from today's Married with Children would not have fit in.

Classic television needs to make a comeback as a viable source of healthy entertainment for the family. The shows that were enjoyable for the entire family, the wholesome story lines, and the absence of sex and violence would help reinstate a moral tone to the entertainment we watch at home.

"Writing is easy: all you do is sit staring at the blank sheet of paper until the drops of blood form on your forehead."

Gene Fowler

Bilingual Education

Michael Bannister

English 1102/In-Class Argument

The United States has always been a nation of immigrants. This is still true today. In the past several decades, more and more people have been coming to the U.S. from Latin America. Most of these people only speak Spanish. Consequently, a tremendous strain has been put on the U.S. public school system as it tries to accommodate the children of these immigrants. To help these children learn English and integrate into American society, many schools with large numbers of immigrant children are offering bilingual classes. Bilingual classes, or bilingual education, consist of a bilingual instructor teaching classes in both the students' native language, usually Spanish, and English throughout the day. The instructor teaches some subjects in one language, and he/she teaches different subjects in the other language. Proponents of bilingual education feel that bilingual classes allow students to learn both English and other subjects being taught because they are unlike "sink-or-swim" English-only classes where students spend so much time attempting to understand what is being said that they do not learn the subject matter. Unfortunately, bilingual classes have failed to perform in practice. Therefore, bilingual education is an ineffective tool for teaching non-native speakers how to speak English.

One of the major problems with bilingual education is that students in bilingual classes have little incentive to learn English. Since the classes are taught in two languages students do not need to know English to understand much of what is being said. Even when students do not understand what is being said, they can receive answers to their questions in Spanish. Hence, because knowledge of English is not needed to survive in these primarily Spanish classes, few students feel the need to learn English, so most don't. Only 5% of students in bilingual classes in California move to English-only classes each year. That means that after twelve years of school less than 50% of students originally in a bilingual class will have learned English. Many simply drop out, realizing they are not going to learn anything. These students, unable to communicate with the rest of the inhabitants of their new country, are effectively doomed to a life of poverty.

Bilingual classes are also very expensive. Schools must offer both bilingual and English-only versions of the same classes, creating paperwork and complicating schedules. Also, teachers for bilingual classes are harder to find than English-only instructors because they must speak a second language as well as have a teaching degree. In some parts of California, the shortage of properly qualified teachers has gotten so bad that schools are hiring persons to act as teachers whose only qualification is the ability to speak a second language. As a result, it is not hard to imagine what sort of education students receive from these untrained teachers.

Bilingual education has failed miserably. Students often end up languishing in classes for years, never learning anything or never moving on to English-only classes. The quality of instruction in bilingual classes is also poor, worsening an already bad situation. The parents of many students eligible to be in bilingual classes realize just how bad such classes can be. For example, a 1996 survey showed that 81% of primarily Spanish-speaking parents did not want their children in bilingual classes. Rather than helping immigrant children learn how to speak English, bilingual education has become a dumping ground for students deemed hopeless by their school system.

♦ ♦ ♦

Persuasive Business Letter

Kelly Yount

English 1102

March 3, 1998

Mr. Jack Wilson
Assistant to the Mayor of Atlanta
55 Trinity Avenue
Atlanta, GA 30335

Dear Mr. Wilson:

As a citizen of Atlanta, I have a growing concern regarding the Chattahoochee River pollution problem. Liveable Planet, of which I am a member, is organizing a panel discussion to focus public awareness on the plight of the Chattahoochee River. This is an invitation for you to join in this panel discussion.

Liveable Planet is pleased to have obtained commitments from Marilyn Szabo, a geology professor at Emory who specializes in water pollution, and from Dan Sheinberg, an engineer with the Atlanta Water Department, to serve on the panel. To complete our panel we are seeking someone from the construction industry and a representative from the mayor's office. This project has also been well received by the Atlanta media, and they have agreed to cover the event.

We cordially extend to you an invitation to participate on this four-member panel which will take place on May 6 at 8:00 p.m. at Georgia State University. As you know, the local news has been crucifying the City of Atlanta and, particularly, the mayor's office with charges ranging from total ineptitude to gross mismanagement of the water department. We believe this panel will provide an excellent forum from which the City of Atlanta can express positive solutions to a very ugly problem.

Mr. Wilson, your participation and knowledge will enlighten us on this growing pollution problem. I look forward to hearing from you by April 1. Thanks for your attention to this matter.

Sincerely,

Kelly L. Yount

cc: Mayor Bill Campbell

Persuasive Business Letter

Whitney A. Whanger

English 1102

April 8, 1998

Herman Weil
Vice President, Southeast Division
Kaiser Foundation Health Programs
9 Piedmont Center
3495 Piedmont Road
Atlanta, Georgia 30305

Dear Mr. Weil:

As a Kaiser Permanente policy holder, I am writing to inform you of my displeasure to learn that my policy does not provide for chiropractic health care.

Recently, I fell and hurt my back. As a result of that injury, I first consulted my primary care physician for treatment. His suggested method involved administering a prescription for pain combined with wearing a back brace for a specified period. Due to my reluctance to take the drugs prescribed, the physician recommended I consult a Doctor of Chiropractic for treatment. Upon my first visit to the chiropractor, I was informed that my present health care policy does not cover chiropractic health care. Following my initial consultation with the chiropractor, I elected to continue with this treatment at my own expense. The treatment included only a few visits to successfully remedy my condition. The pain I was experiencing lessened considerably immediately following the first visit and I soon fully recovered without the need to take even an aspirin for the pain, much less the initial prescription for serious drugs suggested by the primary care physician. I understand that not all insurance companies provide chiropractic health care coverage due to the fact that it is a relatively new alternative treatment method and that the general public is still somewhat uneducated as to benefits this type of care offers in many cases. Many do not realize that chiropractors receive a doctorate degree following many years of study. While other professed alternative health care providers such as acupuncturists and reflexologists only require minimal training to practice their profession. Raquel Martin explains that "the department of Health and Human services classifies doctors of chiropractic as 'category one'' providers. 'Category one' includes medical doctors, osteopaths and dentists" (Martin 267). If your company covers "category one" providers, why would you exclude chiropractors?

I am also aware that the American Medical Association (AMA) exerts considerable influence over much of the health care industry including health care insurance providers Unfortunately, this may be one of the reasons why many policies do not cover chiropractic care. For example, the fact that "the AMA and organized medicine illegally boycotted chiropractors as a profession" leads me to believe that the AMA may be pressuring the health care providers to exclude chiropractic care coverage (Press 116-122). I feel that insurance providers should consider the individual needs of their policy holders instead of allowing the AMA to dictate their plan options.

In spite of the general unawareness on the part of the public, and the pressures applied by the AMA, chiropractic care has continued to make strides in the health care field over the years and continues to gain acceptance as more and more people seek this alternative treatment with satisfactory results. The time has come for the publicly funded health-care sector to fully explore the potential of chiropractic sciences" (Williams 721). It is becoming increasingly common for patients to choose health care coverage that includes both chiropractic care along with their traditional medical care. For example, a recent survey conducted in Canada found that "97% of chiropractors refer patients to physicians for care and that 84% also had patients referred to them from physicians" (Low).

I recommend that your company reconsider its position in providing chiropractic coverage to your individual policy holders for several reasons. Primarily, offering this coverage would provide your policy holders with the ability to choose the type of care they prefer and/or require depending on the circumstances. It could also provide cost saving benefits to your company. According to one expert. "The Health Care Sector should not be deterred by the economic interest of other health care professions from utilizing chiropractic as a low-cost alternative wherever and whenever appropriate" (Shekelle 394). Chiropractic care focuses on preventative medicine that allows the body to maintain a healthy state through natural methods without the use of harsh and expensive drugs. It allows the body to heal faster with little, if any, time lost due to disability. Since it requires less visits than normally required for medical treatment, it is ultimately less expensive to your company. I discovered first hand that it is not as expensive as medical treatment when I chose to see a chiropractor at my own expense since my current insurance policy does not cover this type of care. It is also important to point out to you that since my accident and recent chiropractic treatment, I have investigated the possibly of changing to another insurance company for my health care coverage to one which provides for this type of treatment. My investigation revealed that several of your competitors do provide for chiropractic care. While I do not choose to make a change in insurance carriers, I will be forced to do so if your current policy continues to eliminate this alternative health care treatment as an option.

Sincerely,

Whitney A. Whanger
Kaiser Permanente Policy Holder 123456789-WAW

Exit Essay

Diane Bita Minsili

ENSL 017

Topic: Identify something that has happened this year to change you.

Each year there is always something that happens in our lives and has an impact on us for the years after. It can be a job promotion, success with an exam, or the death of someone we loved. Last year the most important thing that happened to me was that Bemire, my best friend, died from AIDS.

The first day of January of last year started in an ordinary manner. I went to Bemir's house so that we could go to school together as usual. When I arrived, she was not waiting for me in the living room as she usually did. I climbed the stairs in a hurry, a little bit angry because I thought that we would be late to school. Bemir was not even dressed; she was lying in bed and looking at the ceiling. She didn't even look at me when I came into her room. I immediately understood that something was wrong with her, and I just sat down to wait for her to tell me. She didn't say anything for five minutes, but then she suddenly looked at me and said, "I have AIDS." At first, I thought it was a joke, I even laughed. However, her look was so sincere that I stopped laughing. Then I started to shiver and said, "No! It's impossible. Bemir, you are joking, right?" She didn't answer and just kept looking at me. Then she explained to me that one of her boyfriends told her that he had AIDS; therefore, she decided to get an AIDS test. She even did it twice, but it was positive both times. I started to cry. I was horrified and devastated. I loved Bemir, and now I would lose her. The history of our friendship flashed through my mind like a dream.

Bemir and I had known each other for a very long time. The first time we met was at school when we were ten. We immediately liked each other and became inseparable. We were more than sisters. We liked the same kinds of clothes music, and even boys. After graduating from primary school, we even decided to go to the same secondary school so that we'd still be together. Bemir was my best friend, and we used to support each other in every situation. However, there was one thing that I always questioned about her: she had too many boyfriends, and that was killing her now.

After I knew that Bemir was ill, I first had the same reaction people usually have against people who have AIDS; I rejected her. However, after some time, we became closer than ever. She was getting sicker every day, and she even stopped going to school. After ten long months, Bemir died in her sleep. Nevertheless, she kept her courage until the end.

Having my best friend die because of AIDS has changed me a lot. I hate that illness more than ever. It has become my worst enemy. However, to fight it, I must know it very well. Therefore, I have read everything I could about AIDS; I have even discovered many things I didn't know about the disease before. At the beginning of 1998, I joined an organization that fights against AIDS. I will feel relieved the day that this horrible disease is completely destroyed, and I hope that this day will come soon.

"The art of writing is the art of discovering what you believe."

David Hare

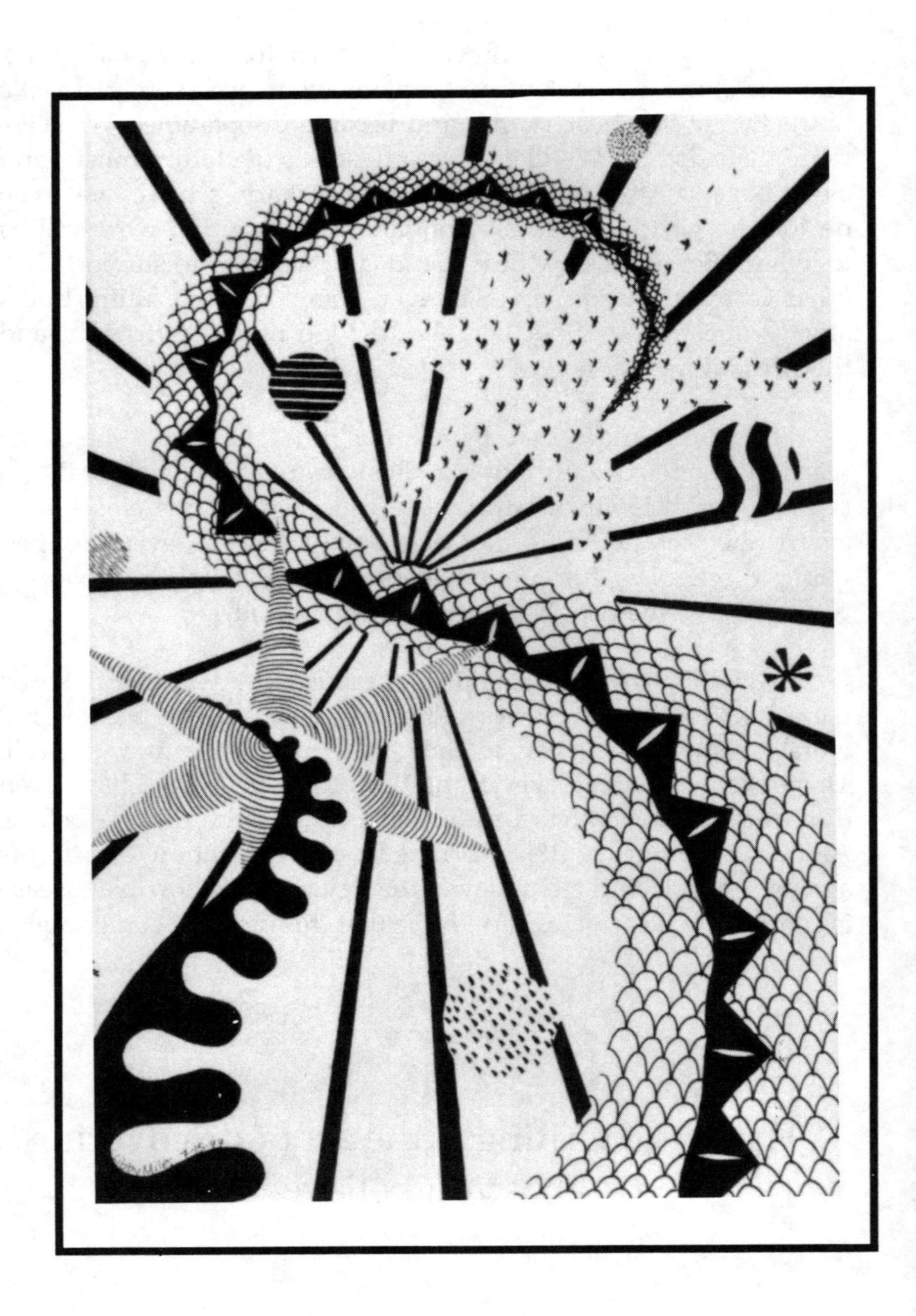

Exit Essay

Paige Eberhart

English 0099

Topic: Characteristics of a party that is out of control.

The time was six o'clock, and I had already started preparing for the big night that was ahead of me. It was the night of my twenty-first birthday, and I wanted to make sure that everything was perfect. I invited everyone that I knew to come to my house to celebrate my big night, including my friends from high school and college. My parents had given me permission to use the house for the event. Soon, everyone would arrive to celebrate my birthday with me, but little did I know what I was about to encounter. I learned that a party is out of control when people who are not invited come anyway, when people at the party are disrespectful of the host's property, and when police officers come to break the party up.

Keeping a party under control is extremely important because it is almost impossible to calm a party once it is out of control. One very important step is to make a list of people who are to be invited and send invitations only to them. Then, the people who are invited can RSVP. If this step is not taken and the host tells everyone about the party, then people who are not invited will show up; in fact, people that the host does not even know will come to the party because they will assume that the party is open invitation so everyone who comes will be welcome. This party could get out of hand because the number of people at the party could double from the original guest list. Also, if the host does not know everyone at the party, this situation could be dangerous because the host is letting absolute strangers, whom he knows nothing about, into the house. As the number of people increases as the night goes on, the party could get very rowdy and loud, and then it could be impossible to break the crowd up. Some people may even raid a party because they may be enemies of the party's host. It is very important for the host to make sure he or she knows exactly who has been invited and who is coming to the party.

Moreover, the host must trust his or her friends well enough to have then over to the house. Sometimes, friends may be disrespectful. When teenagers are in a large group, they may do terrible things just to get attention from their peers. Some teens may think that they can get attention by trashing the house. They think that since the house is not theirs, they do not have to worry about cleaning up the mess that they make. For example, if a party is going on and someone spills a drink, he or she may not even bother to clean the mess up but rather leave it for the house's owner to deal with. Also, if friends are not very respectful, they may be likely to steal as well. It is very difficult to be a security guard and a good host at one's own party; therefore, someone can easily go into one of the bedrooms in the house and steal a bracelet or earrings and wear this jewelry right out of the house. If a party gets out of control, people may park in the owner's yard since there is no other parking available. These cars leave terrible tire tracks in the yard and really damage the lawn. A host must be sure that friends are really friends when inviting them to such an event.

Lastly, it is easy to tell that a party is out of control when the police show up. A party could very well get out of hand just by being too loud. Neighbors may even call the police because of the noise, which disrupts their sleep. Police officers usually come to parties to make sure that everything is under control but may feel that the gathering is not under control, so at this point the police are needed to break up the party. Also, illegal activities, such as providing alcohol to minors, may be going on. The minors may then leave the party and try to drive home while they are under the influence of alcohol. Because they are minors, they are under the legal age for alcohol consumption; in addition, they are driving while drunk. Cops should come in this situation because they are the only ones who can stop this from happening and get the party under control.

Obviously, keeping a party under control is very important. It is easy to let bad situations pass by when people are having a good time, and it is hard to be the host and keep the party under control too. But to keep a party under control and to make it successful, hosts must take several precautions, such as making a guest list, inviting only trusted friends, and giving the police no reason to show up; once these steps have been implemented, the party should go very smoothly.

◆◆◆

"If you can teach me a new word,
I'll walk all the way to China
to get it."

Turkish Proverb

Exit Essay

Jennifer Graybeal

English 0099

Topic: The animal that makes the worst apartment pet.

Many people throughout America find that owning a pet can be great for companionship. A pet, such as a dog, is excellent for spending time with. But one must be sure to obtain the right dog for the environment. For instance, if a person chooses to live in an apartment, having a large dog might not be suitable. A large dog can be the worst apartment pet because it requires lots of space to live, can cause odor problems, and can often be disturbing to the neighbors.

A large dog is not provided the space it needs to live properly in an apartment. Apartments are often small and cause a dog to feel claustrophobic. Large dogs need a big grassy place where they can stretch their legs and run. Without access to a proper living environment, large dogs are not able to obtain the exercise they need to live healthfully.

Another problem is that many people work nine-to-five jobs, so their dogs are left at home alone. Without an owner present, the dog is not provided with the proper care. No one is there to let the dog out for bathroom privileges. When the owner returns home, he/she may have to clean up a wonderful surprise. Since an apartment is smaller than most homes, the smell from such surprises can be quite unpleasant.

Lastly, a large dog in an apartment is often disturbing to neighbors. Living in an apartment complex, one will encounter lots of neighbors. Some neighbors, however, will not be fond of large dogs. For instance, if a person has a large dog and lives next door to a person without one, the dog owner may encounter a conflict. The neighbor may complain about the dog's barking at night. In addition, the neighbor might complain that the dog barks at arriving guests.

Having a large dog at an apartment complex can be quite a hassle. Not only is the dog lacking the proper environment, but the dog also lacks the proper care as well. A large dog is not suitable for an apartment because it is not given proper space to live, can cause bad odor problems, and can be quite disturbing to neighbors. Therefore, it is essential that a large dog owner takes into consideration the environment before he or she chooses to live in an apartment.

♦ ♦ ♦

"It has been said that writing comes more easily if you have something to say.

Sholem Asch

Exit Essay

Danielle Grillaert

English 0099

Topic: Characteristics of a party that is out of control.

Parties happen all of the time for different reasons such as birthdays, graduations, and fun. Sometimes these parties can get a little crazy. Even though parties are supposed to be a way for people to relax and have fun, many times these gatherings can get out of control.

Many parties start out slow with very few people invited, but often people who are not invited show up, especially at teen parties. Teenagers whose parents have gone out of town throw many of the parties that get out of control. At these parties most of the time drugs and/or alcohol are present. When teenagers hear about a party where alcohol is being served, they probably will tell their friends about this party. Often these teens will show up at a party to which they were not invited. With so many people at the party, this party may get out of control.

With the over-crowding in an enclosed space, many of the partygoers get drunk and often get a little rowdy. Sometimes fights break out at these parties. These fights usually start as a result of a simple accident. For instance, if there is dancing at the party and one boy accidentally bumps into another, sometimes a fight will start. Even though bumping into each other was an accident, tempers often get out of control when alcohol is involved. During the resulting fights, sometimes items in the house may be broken. Also, partygoers often move furniture around in order to create a dance floor or just for extra space for mixing. Sometimes this furniture gets broken or stained.

Although these occurrences are accidents, the party has gotten out of control.

Along with fights occurring and the host's items being broken, most of the time parties get loud. When people are having fun, they do not realize how loud they are. Many times parties get so loud that the parties disturb a neighbor. Occasionally the neighbor will call the host and ask him or her to quiet the party down; however, when a party gets too loud for the host to control, the gathering is then out of control. At this point the police might come and ask the partygoers to quiet down or simply break the party up. Obviously, once the police have been called, the party is definitely out of control.

People like to relax and have fun, and often going to a party is the answer. But sometimes the partygoers get carried away. Parties can easily get out of control, especially when everyone there is having fun.

♦♦♦

"The reason a writer writes a book
is to forget a book and
the reason a reader reads one
is to remember it."

Thomas Wolfe

Exit Essay

Jennifer Jones

English 0099

Topic: The television show that has affected Americans in significant ways.

When rating a television show that has significantly affected Americans, one has to consider several factors. It is necessary to look at both the positive and negative feedback from all audiences. A show that has been viewed more negative than positive is *Beavis and Butthead.* This show displays nothing but bad scenarios, bad behavior, and explicit language.

For one, the scenarios of this television series are nothing but damaging to the mind. The two characters perform activities that are both inappropriate towards animals and humans. They also perform random acts of violence on each other, acts that result in injury, and then they laugh at their injuries, such as a broken arm. Anybody knows that when a person breaks an arm, that person does not laugh nor think that the injury is funny; rather, the person experiences agony. These characters and their stunts mislead the viewers and can cause a viewer to perform the action. For example, one little boy, after watching the show, used matches to set a fire which burned down his family's house. He got this idea from *Beavis and Butthead.* If the writers, producers, and actors would only give these scenarios more thought, they may change the story line, so some of these real-life incidents may not occur.

Another inappropriate aspect of this show is the behavior that it displays. This behavior consists of rudeness to each other, neighbors, and friends, all leading to unnecessary arguments with each other. Because of Beavis' and Butthead's age, they should be attending high school, possibly driving, and holding a part-time job, but their immature behavior causes them to fail their classes, not pass their driving tests, and do a slack job at work and get fired. In their spare time they do nothing but torture each other in some harmful way or simply watch TV all day. However, if Beavis and Butthead are doing poorly in school and don't work too much, then I don't see how they have the money for their nice house, which they trash, or the money to buy beer. Their behavior has influenced viewers to perform the same stunts as Beavis and Butthead do and believe that they will not experience any negative effects.

A third negative aspect of this show is the bad language involved. As a child, one picks up inappropriate words. Watching a show and listening to every word, viewers will notice that every two to four words are a cuss word. This type of language is the kind that many parents prefer that their children not use, so the parents make the children either cut off the TV or change the program. The language causes children to get into trouble for something that they thought was okay to say and did not expect any negative consequences for using. If the writers were to take out every cuss word in this television show or change it to suitable language for young viewers, the show would improve, but it would still have a negative impact on viewers.

Overall, this show displays very few positive outcomes because of its bad case scenarios, immature behavior, and inappropriate language. If I had the power to have this show taken off of the air, I would because of the overall misconceptions the show gives viewers about what is "cool" and what isn't.

Actual Alternate Regents' Exam

David Ajoy

TOPIC: How do you expect your college education to change the rest of your life?

Every day one of the most powerful television companies, NBC, broadcasts one or more public service announcements, and recently, it started showing celebrities and well-known people giving viewers a few words of encouragement to stay in school. President Clinton, in his last State of the Union address, emphasized the importance of education, and Georgia Governor Zell Miller has made of the Hope Scholarship program a paradigm to be followed by other states. It seems, based on these few examples, that education, and especially college education, is a very important and positive way to improve ourselves and reach our goals. College education gives us important tools to deal with life, increases the quality of jobs that we will be able to have, and improves our overall knowledge to make us better human beings.

Now that I have been going to college for a year, I can easily mention a few tools that this kind of education has given me. The combination of work and studies has improved my sense of responsibility, and the sometimes challenging assignments have made me realize that every barrier can be breached. Time has become one of the most valuable things, but its scarcity has given me the tool of organization. Getting a college education has changed my life already, and in the following years, it will increase my patience and persistence as I get closer to graduation.

It is not a surprise that high-paying jobs are related to the skills and abilities of the employees. Especially in a capitalist country such as the United States, companies do not want to hire people if the individuals cannot do the tasks that they are required to do. On the same basis, people with a higher degree of education are most likely to be hired for positions that pay higher salaries. Thus, a college education becomes a valid way of gaining financial well-being.

A college education also improves our overall knowledge. Most majors include courses of English, history, ethics and psychology. Even though these may not be directly related to the specific course of study that students are interested in, these subjects serve the purpose of increasing students' overall knowledge, and most importantly, these courses are intended to persuade the students to apply that knowledge. By these means, a college education helps students become more objective and releases them from prejudices.

It is not the intention of NBC, President Clinton, nor Governor Miller to advertise and promote education only because it sounds good. A college education has many advantages attached. Not only will it change our future, but it will also create a society with people that can deal with life more easily, an economy handsomely reflected in its individuals, and a spirit of very humane people.

◆◆◆

"Of every four words I write,
I strike out three."

Nicolas Boileau

Practice Regents' Essay Exam

Ashley Abercrombie

English 1102/Honors

Topic: What are the chief reasons for our youth's interest in music videos? Explain.

Ever since MTV first aired on cable television, it has experienced tremendous popularity, especially with the younger part of the population. Not only could people listen to their favorite music, but they could also see and experience more of what the music was about. Today, several other channels specializing in the viewing of music videos are also enjoying enormous popularity. Young people are especially fascinated by music videos because they display standards of social acceptance and current fashion and influence personal expression.

To many, high fashion goes hand in hand with the world of music videos and rock and roll. Madonna, for example, is legendary in American culture and is admired the world over. She is not only a talented performer, but also a standard of current fashion. She can appear risque, innocent, elegant or sexy at any given time; she always holds the eye of the public because of her personal flair for style. Several other trends among teenagers may not have existed had it not been for music channels. The so-called grunge look, for instance, was popularized mostly by such alternative bands as Nirvana, Pearl Jam, and Soundgarden from Seattle. This style changed fashion drastically among young people; soiled, oversized, or thrift store clothing as well as unkempt hair became prevalent.

Most young people in our nation have an overwhelming desire to express themselves as individuals. People such as the artist formerly known as Prince exude this characteristic. Most artists who are remotely appreciated by the public demonstrate their uniqueness. Sinead O'Connor's baldness was a feature that received much publicity. The Red Hot Chili Peppers attract an audience by exhibiting their flamboyance and raciness through their flashy clothing and untamed instrumental and lyrical styles. Teenagers can relate to these displays of individualism and outrageousness; as a result, teenagers watch MTV and other music channels.

To many, the teenage years are filled with insecurities over relationships, appearances, and popularity. In contrast, music videos consist of artists who exude self-confidence and who have achieved extreme success because they are liked by the public, they are highly talented, and often, they are astoundingly beautiful. By watching these videos, teenagers come closer to the characteristics they admire in their favorite artists. For example, Sheryl Crow has recently topped the charts with her new album and had a number one video at the same time. She is a stunning, ultra-thin, glamorous brunette with a unique voice that fascinates her audience. Her lyrics address themes that young people can relate to; at the same time, she is adored by thousands of men. Young women desire to be more like her, and men just desire her, causing demand for her video to be aired several times a day.

"There is no way of writing well
and also of writing easily."

Laurence Sterne

Practice Regents' Essay Exam

Scott Campbell

English 1102

TOPIC: Have computers made our lives easier or more complicated? Explain.

Computers are a major part of our present-day society. It is hard nowadays to find a job that does not involve computers to some extent. Computers can perform tasks quicker and more efficiently than previous methods. However, there are still those individuals who claim that computers complicate life more than they help. Yet, through a simple consideration of computers' roles in our society, we can clearly see that computers are a vital aide in our world today.

The first place one can look to see the helpful aspects of computers is in the business world. Computers perform numerous tasks for many different types of businesses. For example, before computers, businesses would have to have large file cabinets to store records and information. Now in place of those bulky file cabinets, a small disk is used to store all of that vital information. Not only do computers save space in the business world, but they also save time. Computers allow businesses to process information in a fraction of the time it would take for people to do it by hand. Moreover, businesses can access any information that they might need with the simple click of a few buttons. While it is true that people must take the time to learn how to use computers properly, it is obvious that, overall, computers make life in the business world much easier.

The next place we can look to see the positive effects of computers is in the average person's life. Computers open all sorts of opportunities to people in their everyday lives. Instead of spending countless hours at the library for a research project, a person only has to surf the Internet to find more than enough information for the average paper. People can also use computers to communicate with other people and to express their own ideas to the world. For example, the Internet offers individuals a medium to open web sites that represent their personal interests and views, but it also allows them access to web sites that represent differing opinions. Computers open many other doors for people once they take the time to learn how to use these devices to their full potential.

Obviously, computers do make our lives easier rather than more complicated. Computers provide an efficient and accurate method of communication, and save time and energy while conserving space. The people who complain that computers are complicating our lives are more often than not the same people who will not take the time to learn how to use computers correctly. Once an individual learns how to use computers, it is amazing how many opportunities are opened and how much time and energy can be saved.

◆◆◆

"Writing is one of the easiest things; erasing is one of the hardest."

Rabbi Israel Salanter

Practice Regents' Essay Exam

Bernice Manning

English 1101

Topic: Does society accept females in roles traditionally held by men more readily than society accepts men in roles traditionally held by women?

I grew up during the Virginia Slims days when it was not fashionable for a woman to smoke in public. I remember the feminist movement and the rights that were fought for. So each time I encounter a delivery woman on the elevator, I am reminded of just how much women have gained. However, it is apparent to me that while society allows women readily to assume what were once male roles, it is difficult to find males in what are traditionally feminine roles.

It is quite common to see a woman driving a tractor-trailer truck these days. For years, women were considered to be less than adequate drivers, and most of us know that a person must have excellent driving skills in order to operate a large truck. But many women have obviously mastered the skill because we see many women driving buses as well as trucks. On the other hand, while women have transitioned into this career, not many men have crossed over into the female-dominated area of nursing. It is still not common to see a male nurse in a hospital or doctor's office. When in the hospital, some people feel more comfortable with a female nurse. In nursing homes a majority of the nurses are female; however, the attendants are mostly male.

While society readily accepts a woman delivering mail, it does not generally place a male in the role of a receptionist. Most businesses endorse having attractive young women to sit at a front desk and greet customers. However, few receptionists or secretaries are men. I think it would be nice to walk in to a place of business and be greeted by a young attractive man. Men are quite capable of assuming these roles and answering the telephone. Moreover, many men have pleasant personalities and voices.

Finally, women are hired to do construction work on the highways and houses; however, seldom is a male hired to do housework. Other than doing handiwork around the house, men are not generally placed in household positions. I believe men would be assets in such positions. After all, most men want clean, tidy houses. Many husbands already perform such household duties as mopping and vacuuming the floors. In fact, some men do housework much better than their spouses. Therefore, men could make a living as domestic engineers.

Obviously, the women's movement did much to bring about changes for women. As a result, women occupy many jobs formerly performed by males only. However, men are not privileged with the same standards because they still have not infiltrated traditional female roles.

♦ ♦ ♦

"The writer does the most, who gives his reader the most knowledge and takes from him the least time."

Samuel Johnson

Practice Regents' Essay Exam

Brian Yates

English 1102

TOPIC: Have computers made our lives easier or more complicated? Explain.

People in the world today are, on the whole, lazier than the generation before them. A person born into the world today has many things that the generation before him or her did not have, such as microwaves, CD players, and, most importantly, computers. The computer can do many things for many different people. For example, a twelve-year-old child uses a computer to play games while a forty-year-old man uses a computer to run his business. Computers make research, communication, and business much easier.

Computers can add many more dimensions and sources to one's research. In the past, many people bought volumes of encyclopedias, yet now all of the volumes can be placed on a single CD. On this CD, there are thousands of pictures, video clips, and music. All of these dimensions add to research. In addition to the encyclopedia, one can also use computers to find books. To illustrate, one can simply type in a key word, and many books with subjects pertaining to that word are listed on the screen. Also, there are millions of magazine and journal articles that can be found on a web site like GALILEO. Consequently, computers make the whole research process easier.

Not only can one use a computer to make the whole research process easier, but one can also use a computer to communicate. With a modem and a telephone line, a person is connected to the world. "The world is a mouse click away" is not an exaggeration. A person can write to another person halfway around the world without picking up a pencil. The instrument the person uses is called electronic mail (E-mail). With E-mail, a person can talk to anyone in the world, and then that person can respond at his or her leisure. In addition to writing people, computers can help users meet new people. People can go to different chatrooms, each with a different topic, and meet new people with the same interests as them. For example, a basketball fan can go into a NBA chatroom and talk to other basketball fans across the country. A computer can link people with similar interests, even if they live in different parts of the world.

In addition to helping individuals communicate, computers can also help businesses in many ways. Computers can help make businesses work better. For instance, businesses used to have big file cabinets to hold different files, and now all they have to do is save this material on computers. A company can also be connected to the world with a web page. Many companies do not even have an office because they do all of their work from computers. Computers, in addition, help businesses keep productivity high by automating machines and collating data. Computers do not need breaks or pay, and they can work twenty-four hours a day. As a result, the many benefits of computers can help make businesses better.

Therefore, computers make people's lives better. Computers help make research less time-consuming, and computers make communication easier for people all over the world. In addition, computers can help companies improve productivity and make millions. Computers make a lot of things easier and better, and they will continue to do so in the future.

Actual Regents' Exam

Ryan P. Fields

Rating: 3

Topic: Explain why you do or do not vote.

The right to vote, given to all citizens over the age of eighteen, is a right that has been argued, studied, and written about. It is a right given to us by the Constitution, but its literal interpretation means many different things to different individuals. The main issue is whether or not to exercise your right to vote when election time comes. While some people choose to remain silent and not exercise this right, I fall on the other side of the issue, maintaining a stance that it is one of the most important rights we are given. Through analyzing the positive effects of voting, I will explain my views and discuss why I choose to vote, the importance of it and its positive effect.

As mentioned earlier, the right to vote is a Constitutional right of all citizens over eighteen. It is a process in which we choose our civic leaders, representatives, and "voice" in government. I believe this process to be one of the most important issues we have, which is why I strongly support voting and all of its properties. It is the most democratic of all government processes -- the people are called upon to make a choice for who will represent them on critical issues, defend their particular views, and speak for them. This alone could be reason enough for exercising this valuable right, but there is more. I choose to vote in elections so that I can voice my support and have input into the governmental process. It is beyond my comprehension the notion of either not wanting to voice an opinion, no caring enough to cast a vote, or simply not taking advantage of this Constitutional privilege.

Many detractors to this idea, or put more simply, the non-voters, argue that their one vote could not possibly make a difference in something as large as a political election. To this, I would argue that every vote counts just as much, and that it is a large collection of single votes that gives victory to a candidate. Also, for non-voters taking this stance, I argue that if one does not place a vote, then he or she gives up any right to complain, voice a harsh opinion, or have any logical argument for how a certain elected individual is doing his or her job.

The voters of our society, and I strongly place myself into this category, see the right to vote as an integral, concrete duty to ourselves, our families, and our society. By the voter's choice, we are given government; and this particular point cannot be more clearly put -- our government, our civic leaders, are put into office by our decisions. Individuals who ignore their right are offering nothing in the overall scheme of this process. Their voices are silent, their choices and views, no matter how coherent, will go unnoticed and unrecognized. On the other hand, voters like myself will have their views both counted and noticed, regardless of the election's outcome. Citizens who choose to vote play a much more crucial role in society than do the more sedentary non-voters simply because they have an opinion they want to express. The non-voters may have an opinion, but unless they cast a vote, it is ignored. Society, being a democratic entity, depends heavily on the voter. If everyone took the position of the non-voters, expressing apathy for the process, our system could not exist. I feel this right is the most important of all rights if we are to maintain the democratic society we sometimes take for granted.

It is common to have arguments over issues in the world today. We argue over little things as well as big, but to me, the argument of whether or not to vote is a very one-sided issue. The advantages of placing a ballot in the ballot box far outweigh the disadvantages. Citizens who cast their singular vote are contributing to a society that needs that vote to continue. I remain religious to the positive effect of the voting right and all of its attributes. The view that voting has no effect is one I simply cannot understand, for not expressing your views is not having a voice -- and in today's world, a voice is a very valuable thing to have.

♦ ♦ ♦

"More than kisses,
letters mingle souls."

John Donne

Actual Regents' Essay Exam

Kristin Mercer

Rating: 4

Topic: Should high school students go steady? Discuss why or why not.

Many parents believe that high school students should not go steady because of the pressures associated with being young, such as sex, drugs, and the struggle for independence. On the contrary, students should go steady in high school for three reasons: security, experience, and partnership. Being in a relationship has the major benefit of learning about other people; thus, the knowledge acquired from a relationship will help teenagers in social situations later in life.

One of the major reasons for going steady is for security. Since many teenagers feel as though their self-esteem is on a roller coaster, they find comfort in knowing that someone will be there for them. For example, after a long day at work, a person tends to feel stressed and tense. Therefore, another individual, such as a boyfriend or girlfriend, can make him or her feel better in a few minutes simply because the individual understands the other person so well. Having a close friend helps many teenagers because they have someone whom they can trust and believe will be there tomorrow or the next day. This feeling of security transfers to self-confidence, and this newfound self-confidence can keep many teens from depression, suicide, drug use, or other dangerous situations.

In addition to security, another reason high school students should go steady is for the experience. Certain natural adolescent curiosities exist in both males and females; having a steady girlfriend or boyfriend minimizes the number of partners for a teenager. As a result of less contact between different partners, there is less of a risk for a teenager to contract a sexually transmitted disease (STD). Also, since many teenagers feel they must be sexually active to fit in, having a steady partner will help curb feelings of doubt, depression, and inferiority, all of which may accompany a one-night stand. In addition to sexual experience, a steady relationship can aid a person later in life. For instance, a steady relationship usually lasts for a significant amount of time; thus; it can provide both partners an opportunity to learn not only about another person but also about himself or herself. This experience helps people decide what they want in a mate and, therefore, can help them in other relationships.

Finally, the most important reason for high school students to go steady is for the partnership. Being in a relationship for a significant amount of time fosters growth and learning. The partners help each other develop emotionally; in turn, this development will help in much of their adult life. For example, a relationship helps teach both partners about sharing and respect. The lessons of responsibility and respect for another person gained in a steady relationship help a person in all facets of life, whether it be at a job, in school, or in a marriage.

Therefore, although a steady relationship in high school may not last until college or even until summer, the benefits of being with a single partner outweigh the improbable benefits of dating around. Being in a relationship helps a person grow individually; ironically, this individual growth helps a person join with others in a union. A relationship can teach so much because of the impact it has on a young person whose very struggle for independence can lead to a safer, more responsible relationship with another individual. Due to the benefits associated with going steady, such as security, experience, and partnership, a student can begin paving the way to adult life while still in high school.

◆ ◆ ◆

Actual Regents' Essay Exam

Marina M. Veal

Rating: 3

Topic: Beauty contests, despite criticism, are still very popular. In your opinion, what are the chief reasons for their popularity? Explain.

With the return of feminism during the twentieth century in the United States, many popular cultural activities came under attack for portraying women as objects. One such activity was the beauty pageant, an event built around beautiful women parading down a runway in bathing suits and evening gowns. Critics of this American pastime contend that women will never achieve full equality with men in society until they take a stand against participating in entertainment that demeans female intelligence in the eyes of men. Yet, despite this valid argument, beauty pageants continue to be very popular due to the American values that sustain their enduring appeal.

Research conducted by renowned sociologists consistently demonstrates that physical attractiveness is highly valued by the American public. Even babies are more attracted to beautiful faces, so it is little wonder that beauty pageants remain so popular with adults. Pageants reward "the most beautiful" creatures America has to offer with lavish attention and financial awards. This is no different than what already occurs each day in regular companies where the most attractive job applicant often receives the reward of a job. Pageants appeal to this unconscious value that society places on superficial beauty.

Another value influencing the enduring tradition of beauty pageants is that of freedom. America was founded on this principle, and its citizens still guard this idea tenaciously some two hundred years later. Although many people question the worthiness of beauty pageants, they ultimately have to concede that the television networks have the right to produce them and that the women have the right to participate in them. Pageants exemplify the freedom a woman has to achieve a goal in the way she feels is best suited to her unique strengths. As a pageant participant, she has the right to capitalize on her beauty to further her career aspirations and forge an identity as an individual. Conversely, it is interesting to note that cultures with the least freedom are also the only ones to ban beauty pageants.

Most importantly, beauty pageants display the cherished American value of receiving monetary compensation for hard work. Despite the accusations of critics, pageant participants are not brainless plastic dolls; they are extremely talented in drama, dance, and music. However, underneath these talents is the foundation of years of intense work that participants faced as youngsters when other children got to play. Their efforts were eventually compensated through pageants as American society rewarded their hard work.

Undoubtedly, these pageants reflect America's firmly entrenched values of physical attractiveness, freedom, and hard work. Pageant participants are the ultimate capitalists who use their strengths to advance their aspirations for better lives. Despite heated criticism of pageants, this entertainment is here to stay as long as Americans cling tightly to their love of freedom of expression.

Separating Church and State

Kathy Zipperer

English 1101/Argument, Researched

In 1786, the Virginia legislature adopted the Virginia Act. This statute for religious freedom was written by Thomas Jefferson, who considered it to be one of his greatest achievements (Ruthven 303). It is the strongest statement regarding religious freedom ever made:

> No man shall be compelled to frequent or support any religious worship, place, or ministry whatsoever, nor shall be enforced, restrained, molested, or burthened in his body or goods, or shall otherwise suffer, on account of his religious opinion or belief. . . all men shall be free to profess . . . their opinions in matters of religion. (qtd. in Ruthven 303)

The ideas contained in the Virginia Act were later incorporated into the Constitution of the United States. When Thomas Jefferson wrote to the Danbury Baptist Association in 1801, he stated that the Constitution had built "a wall of separation between Church and State" (qtd. in Ruthven 304). Jefferson foresaw a country where reasoning flourished; he anticipated a country free from the "religiously-based tyrannies that had dominated" Europe (Ruthven 305). Jefferson actually believed that the entire country would be Unitarian by the mid-1800's (Smoler 52). The actual consequence of state-supported religious freedom was that many religions and religious denominations flourished. Jefferson and the makers of the Constitution certainly did not intend that the wall of separation between church and state would protect any group that claimed to be a "church" from public or governmental scrutiny. He could not predict the truly commercial society that resulted from the American Revolution (Smoler 52); therefore, he could not foresee churches with tax-free incomes over one billion dollars per year, churches which run multi-billion dollar businesses, or churches which own a1nd operate financial institutions with little interference from government because they claim protection from scrutiny under the First Amendment to the Constitution. Many groups who claim exemption from taxes based on their charitable nature are frequently quite tight-fisted when it comes to actual distribution of their wealth. These groups should not be allowed to hide behind the façade of religiosity in order to be tax-exempt when they are actually doing business as for-profit corporations.

A non-profit corporation is a corporation "that is not organized for the primary purpose of making" a profit (Anosike 51). The IRS describes these businesses as organizations dedicated exclusively to charitable, religious, scientific, literary, or educational purposes; in addition, they must provide services which are beneficial to the public interest (Anosike 57). Almost all churches are non-profit, tax-exempt organizations. Problems arise when non-profits ignore the exclusivity clause and forget that they are acting in the public's interest. This is particularly true for church organizations who tend to view their duty to the public as extending only to their members, their executives, or those people the organization seeks to convert. For example, six Atlanta churches of different denominations have banded together to form a credit union to compete in the commercial banking market. Unlike a credit union formed for employees of a corporation or union, this credit union is formed for the church members. The credit union can offer credit cards, checking accounts, loans, and other benefits (Georgia). Not only do the churches enjoy non-profit, tax-exempt status, but the credit union also does. The Georgia Credit Union Affiliates use a web site to explain why they should keep their tax-exempt status even though they openly state they are directly competing in the commercial, taxable, corporate market. One of the credit union organizers, a minister, hopes that the credit union will be able to make loans in areas of south DeKalb County that have been redlined by traditional banks. In this endeavor, the credit union would not only complement the for-profit commercial establishment, but the minister hopes it would also "augment the area's spiritual power" (Harris). In contrast to the minister's hope for community development and spiritual growth, the marketing director, Steven Strawbridge, is banking on economic growth: "We want to be a major financial institution . . . as big as some of the larger banks" (qtd. in Harris). Clearly, this is a non-profit organization that is now directly competing with for-profit institutions. While the credit union is under considerably more scrutiny by state and federal agencies than the churches it serves, the church leaders and members are the credit union's board of directors. The church leaders, by virtue of their occupations, will serve with an agenda that includes what their god proscribes. Each board member will serve while constantly choosing between what is good for them, their credit union, their church, and their religion. One can only surmise that the South DeKalb churches will use religion as the crucial factor for policy decisions.

Another example of a narrow interpretation of public interest is displayed by Pat Robertson, former Presidential candidate. Anyone who disagrees with the beliefs about God espoused by Robertson's Christian Broadcasting Network (CBN) is the "evil enemy" and "the soldiers of CBN hate the un-American, immoral, and ungodly enemy" (Straub 293). Pat Robertson, while claiming to be a prophet of God, has publicly refuted critics. According to Robertson, the Bible threatens harm to those who criticize or try to silence one of God's prophets (299). Because he arrogantly assumes he has received a mandate from God, he has no restraint in telling people who watch The 700 Club how to vote (301). Using his non-profit business, he influences political choices and actively lobbies for political candidates. As an American citizen, he may choose to do this. However, even though Robertson broadcasts for a non-profit corporation, his primary purpose is religious; therefore, he should not lobby and retain his tax-exempt status. When he crosses from his spiritual world to the real world of United States politics, Robertson violates his charter and the public's trust. As Kenneth Albrecht of the National Charities Information Bureau states, "Nonprofits better get it straight that a not-for-profit has a public service mandate and they mix it up at the peril of the public trust. Without the public trust, the emperor charity has no clothes" (qtd. in Clark 1004).

Moreover, public trust can be and should be a problem for religious-based non-profits. Public sentiment is one of the few restraints on churches and religiously oriented organizations. Public outcry was great when, in the 1970's, a newspaper reported that Boys Town (a Catholic non-profit) spent $6 million per year on their orphanage but owned over $200 million in assets (Clark 989). However, these examples pale in comparison to a cursory examination of The Church of Jesus Christ of Latter-Day Saints. This church owns much of the downtown area of Salt Lake City: the Temple complex, church offices, museums, the Hotel Utah, ZCMI--the city's largest department store, and several office buildings (Ruthven 113). The church offices tower over the Temple complex. While Brigham Young may have found the offices overshadowing the church unacceptable, today it is entirely appropriate since "the Church Corporate is much more powerful than the Church Spiritual," and the priests and elders who run the church offices are corporate executives (113). Ruthven explains,

> The church owns farm lands and urban properties, not just in Utah, but all over the United States. It controls a dozen radio and TV stations, four insurance companies, a newspaper, clothing mills and department stores, as well as investment portfolios worth billions. The full extent of its income is never divulged; but it is thought that its earnings from tithings--from the 25 to 40 per cent [sic] of 'good' Mormons who pay a tenth of their salaries to the Church--runs to almost a billion dollars a year. (113)

This is not a corporation acting in the public interest. This is a religious group acting in its own best interests, amassing wealth, property, and power. If a chemical corporation were operating in this manner, it would be vilified by public sentiment. But, because the Latter Day Saints are able to hide behind the seemingly impenetrable wall of religion, they are not scrutinized by the public or even the U. S. Government (IRS) acting in the public's interest, which is also the government's mandate.

At what point should citizens throw their hand into the air and shout "STOP"? These are only a few examples of religious non-profits gone awry. One can choose any number of televangelists, faithhealers, or other denominational organizations as further illustrations. What is the solution to the problem of non-profits, particularly churches, which are crossing back and forth between religion and secular politics, commercial ventures, and outrageous fortunes? There are currently several pieces of legislation pending in Congress which would restrict non-profits. One bill under consideration limits the income of top executives of charities to $200,000 or the same salary as the United States President (Clark 1003). Another bill, called "The Truth in Tax-Exempt Giving Act," would require non-profits to make financial disclosure available all donors on request and to provide an annual list of all employess earning $100,000 or more (1003). Nevertheless, these are merely band-aids for the problem of churches and religious organizations acting outside the public interst. Legislation with more merit would require all non-profits to provide accurate details of gross income, corporate (administrative) expenses, and the amount of assets that were returned to the public interest. In addition, effective legislation might require 75% of gross income to be spent annually for the public interest.

Because Congress tends to muddle legislation, the best solution would be for church members and religious adherents to scrutinize themselves. Regardless of their spiritual beliefs, citizens that donate their money, property, and time to non-profit organizations must insist that these corporations act ethically. They must insist that administrative costs are minimized and that the programs they are providing, whether it is a voter registration drive or Sunday school, are in the public's interest. Mostly, they must refrain from legislating laws which deny citizens from expressing their opinions in matters of religion or moral matters. A real balance of power between religion and secularism will only be found when the leadership and members of the churches understand that their freedom of religion and their non-profit, tax-exempt corporations thrive because the Constitution guarantees diversity of religion through the wall separating church and state. It protects religious supporters' viewpoints alongside and not at the expense of secular interests.

Works Cited

Anosike, Benji O. How to Form Your Own Profit or Non-Profit Corporation Without a Lawyer. Newark: Do-It-Yourself, 1995.

Clark, Charles S. "Charitable Giving: The Issues." The CQ Researcher 12 Nov. 1993: 987+.

Georgia Credit Union Affiliates. "Statistics and Issues." Georgia's Credit Unions. Online. Mindspring II. Internet. 29 May 1997. Available http://www.gacreditunions.org/statsandissues.html

Harris, Jonathan. "6 Churches Establish Credit Union." Atlanta Journal-Constitution 22 Feb. 1997: D1.

Ruthven, Malise. The Divine Supermarket: Shopping for God in America. New York: Morrow, 1989.

Smoler, Fredric. "The Radical Revolution: An Interview with Gordon Wood." American Heritage Dec. 1992: 51-58.

Straub, Gerard Thomas. Salvation for Sale: An Insider's View of Pat Robertson's Ministry. Buffalo: Prometheus, 1986.

Work Relief and Public Services: Two Birds with One Proposal

Neil Graf

English 1102H/Argumentation, Researched

Many Americans have a hard time finding adequate employment. Before 1997, many unemployed poor Americans received assistance from the federal government through the Aid for Families with Dependent Children (AFDC) program, more commonly known as "welfare." Christopher Jencks describes AFDC as a program providing meager benefits to allow survival for the poorest of the poor, especially single mothers and the disabled. Many of these benefits were also extended to able-bodied workers who could not find employment. The assistance was minimal, usually not even enough to raise recipients above the poverty line. Aid was terminated or lessened as they found employment or other income. Nonetheless, many depended on the food stamps and cash assistance that welfare provided (Jencks 123-4).

In August of 1996, President Clinton signed into law a welfare-reform measure. The new program, called Temporary Assistance for Needy Families (TANF), reduced benefit levels in key programs, such as Food Stamps and Medicaid. More importantly, any able-bodied working age American is now required to find work after two years on the program. After this time, cash benefits are retracted, even if work is unavailable. Furthermore, a person is only eligible for benefits for no more than five years total in a lifetime.

The government wanted to motivate the jobless to seek work, but the reform will fall short. Employment is often scarce, especially for semi-skilled, under-educated workers. Jennifer Wolch suggests that these reforms were chosen by the government because they are easier to implement than an employment-assistance program (2). Now that poverty assistance is virtually out of the hands of the federal government, state and local governments are required to pick up the slack and develop job programs. However, Wolch observes that the states are following the federal model and becoming stingier (2). Programs to develop new jobs are now more essential than ever because the money to help the unemployed is not available anymore. Therefore, a way to aid the poor and the jobless is to provide jobs, especially public-sector jobs.

Still, no notable programs have emerged. J. Eugene Grigsby chides both the government and businesses for not providing jobs in the wake of welfare reform. He notes that despite an expanding economy, semi-skilled jobs are still scarce and those that do exist rarely provide a living wage (2). The reform policy demonstrates irresponsibility on a nationwide scale.

An alternative exists—public works jobs. In the 1930s, Franklin D. Roosevelt's administration implemented huge employment programs to alleviate the shattering effects of the Great Depression. One of these programs was the Works Progress Administration (WPA), which was started in 1935. The WPA provided jobs to many unemployed or underemployed Americans. These were public works jobs that built and repaired the nation's infrastructure on a grand scale. Formerly destitute workers built thousands of roads, schools, sewers, bridges, and other structures, including LaGuardia Airport in New York City. Unlike a cash handout, this was work relief that created good jobs at a decent wage. William Julius Wilson suggests that a program like the WPA could be implemented today, if not by the national government, then by the states to help the new pool of ex-welfare recipients. He claims that it could be an "immediate solution to the jobs problem" (16).

The repair of the infrastructure of Georgia, especially Atlanta, is a pressing need that public workers could meet. Quite a few problems facing the city of Atlanta right now could be resolved by public workers. To employ former welfare recipients to do this type of work is doubly effective in that it gives work to those who need it while improving the community. For example, sewer lines in Atlanta are deteriorating to the point that they explode and leak into the area's water supply. The pollution that these leaks create has gotten national attention. Julie Hairston writes that rather than fix the sewer pipes, the city of Atlanta elects to pay seven million dollars a year in pollution fines to the Environmental Protection Agency (EPA) and the state of Georgia. As a result, sewer rates have been increased by the city government, affecting businesses and consumers, especially tenants in low-rent apartments (1).

A strategy for solving this problem comes from the WPA model. Rather than contracting in the private sector or relying on state agencies, the city of Atlanta could produce its own pool of needy workers to deal with the sewer problem. These workers could be TANF ex-recipients who cannot find jobs elsewhere. The city could train the workers, giving them needed skills. Furthermore, the workers would earn a low, but competitive, wage. After the major sewer repairs were completed, workers would have the option of remaining on the city payroll and performing maintenance. But Wilson maintains that moving onto private sector jobs, depending on availability, might also occur, especially if training is extensive.

Applications of this idea are not limited to sewer work. The deterioration of public schools is a national problem. Areas with a smaller tax base, such as inner cities, tend to have lower quality schools. Opportunities for quality education are reduced if schools are falling apart around the students, one reason why dropout rates are particularly high in inner city neighborhoods. Moreover, an incomplete education often leads to unemployment and, subsequently, to dependence on public aid. Thomas Hale reports that even amongst the poor who do have jobs, lower education leads to a higher possibility of underemployment and continued poverty (2). Therefore, to fix the schools would be a good policy for the governments in the fight against poverty. Like the sewer-repair proposal, the newly created workforce would be perfectly adapted to school repair: a motivated blue-collar workforce designed to repair crumbling infrastructure like old school buildings.

To employ such a workforce would be a multifaceted victory. The workers themselves benefit because they would be gainfully employed and independent. As Wilson points out, working does not have the stigma attached to a cash handout (15). The city would be aided by a large workforce readily available to provide maintenance for schools that really need them. Lastly, the school children would benefit. The gift of a good learning environment is priceless and could help prevent future poverty.

Another way to combat the unemployment problem is to extend public transportation. One reason that work is difficult to find in Atlanta is that many companies have moved to the suburbs, taking with them jobs that semi-skilled inner city residents need to live. This trend has the effect of marginalizing city people, compounding their poverty and joblessness. Before long, a lack of transportation can turn into a lack of motivation to seek needed employment.

While the city proper has a decent transit service, travelling to or from the outlying suburbs can be time-consuming. One of the main reasons is that MARTA, the Metro Atlanta Transit Authority, does not provide the suburbs with rail service. These communities are the fastest growing in the area and, therefore, have need for public transit. These transportation deficiencies result in isolation of the suburbs, such as Gwinnett and Cobb counties experience.

Potentially, inner city workers could build new transit lines. Rail lines to the suburbs or new express lanes on highways for bus service could help city dwellers. Formerly confined to a limited local job market, new mobility would mean more opportunities. These workers would be building their own success. Community morale and individual confidence, the unwritten benefits of good employment, would swell, helping bring poor neighborhoods out of a slump. Stacy Shelton emphasizes the importance of transporting low-wage workers to

Gwinnett County, as well as the traffic and environmental benefits of public transit.

Rail lines have been suggested as a way to connect Atlanta with Cobb and Gwinnett counties, even stretching to Chattanooga and Athens. Urban transit planners are currently doing research on the feasibility of such plans. Shelton writes that the federal government is funding these studies and would subsidize the construction and operation of the lines. It is reasonable to expect the government to use public labor for the project.

The suburbs would receive traffic-free access to the heart of the city and especially to Hartsfield Airport. Wilson writes that every successful suburban area is intricately connected to its central city. Furthermore, when cities lag behind, their suburbs also decline (9). The reason is that successful suburbs need to be located around a city that provides a transportation hub, such as the airport, and business centers, such as Downtown and Buckhead. Also important is a good workforce, much of which the suburbs shut out with inadequate transportation. If the suburbs and the city could work together to increase access, then both areas could benefit immensely. City residents would have access to the growth of the suburbs. The income-based transportation problems would be immediately alleviated, and the convenience of travelling on an efficient commuter line will promote continued use after a job is attained and held.

The need for this type of public employment must be approached as a regional problem. Suburban authorities will be reluctant to solve an urban or even inner-city problem. The problems associated with bad sewers, bad schools, and bad transit are community problems, both from an economic and a moral standpoint. But unless something is done, the infrastructure will continue to crumble, and citizens will remain unemployed. The WPA was very successful, but the federal government seems reluctant to try a similar program today. The problem of finding jobs for welfare recipients is now up to state and local authorities. Urban planners need a positive social and infrastructure-based agenda, not just a tightening of budgets at the expense of the disadvantaged. All can benefit from helping employ the needy.

♦♦♦

Works Cited

Cook, Nathaniel W. "DeKalb Residents Unsure about Commuter Train." The Atlanta Journal-Constitution 12 Mar. 1998: C2.

Grigsby, J. Eugene III. "Welfare Reform Means Business as Usual." Journal of the American Planning Association Winter 1998: 19-21. Periodical Abstracts. Online. 10 Mar. 1998.

Hairston, Julie B. "Sewer Rate Hike Will Raise Cost of Business in City." Atlanta Business Chronicle 31 Jan. 1997: 12A. Ebsco Index. Online. 16 Mar. 1998.

Hale, Thomas W. "The Working Poor." Monthly Labor Review Sept. 1997: 47-48. Periodical Abstracts. Online. 10 Mar. 1998.

Jencks, Christopher. Rethinking Social Policy: Race, Poverty, and the Underclass. New York: HarperPerennial, 1992.

Shelton, Stacy. "Residents Speak Out on Commuter Rail Line." Atlanta Journal-Constitution 11 Mar. 1998: C4.

Wilson, William Julius. "When Work Disappears." Political Science Quarterly Winter 1996-7: 567-95. Periodical Abstracts. Online. 10 Mar. 1998.

Wolch, Jennifer R. "America's New Urban Policy: Welfare Reform and the Fate of American Cities." Journal of the American Planning Association Winter 1998: 8-11. Periodical Abstracts. Online. 10 Mar. 1998.

The Challenge of Reforming Welfare

Linda Norman

English 1102/Argumentation, Researched

As a child I remember that my mother had to have major surgery and was unable to work for several months. She was given sick leave, but her job didn't have disability payments, and after about three weeks, my mother was forced to apply for government food subsidies (the predecessor of food stamps). This was a humiliating experience for my mother who had been taught (as she taught us) that she should work for a living and never accept handouts. We had to make sure that none of the neighbors saw us unloading the food since it was easy to spot the "government grocery bags." This seemed to be a very difficult time for my mother, not because we lacked anything but because she was unable to provide for her children. It may seem that my mother's pride was misplaced based upon the circumstances, but it was this same type of integrity that motivated her generation to get off the welfare rolls as soon as possible. The stigma associated with being a welfare recipient was demeaning to people who believed in providing for their family through honest hard work.

Today the stigma of being a welfare recipient has, in some instances, been replaced by one of pride at "getting one over on all the suckers who work for a living." While most people wonder how anyone, already living at or below the poverty level, could be content with a life that is dependent upon government assistance, the welfare system has made it easy to accept and even exploit this lifestyle. Donald Norris Lyke Thompson state that "welfare is an inadequate response to the problem of poverty; it is perceived to neither increase income enough to end poverty nor encourage its recipients to stand up and leave it on their own" (3-4). The present system has helped to foster an attitude of dependence and penalizes recipients for exceeding income criteria instead of providing them with continued financial support during a transition period. Thus, we see a majority of recipients staying on welfare longer because the alternative is a loss in benefits or a minimum wage job. With the increasing number of recipients and the rising cost of funding welfare, moving people from the welfare rolls and into the workforce has been the focus of the welfare reform issue. Exactly how to achieve this goal was unclear since any reform would require harsh measures, but one thing was certain; something had to be done about the welfare system. President Clinton originally drafted a plan for reform during his first administration. The health care reform issue overshadowed this initial plan, so further work on the bill was delayed. The presidential election stalled the measure again but Congress was determined to pass a welfare reform measure before it adjourned the 104th session. President Clinton strongly opposed several provisions of the bill but would not allow the reform issue to be stalled any longer, so he signed the bill into law. Although The Personal Responsibility and Work Opportunity Reconciliation Act of 1996 was enacted to discourage and eliminate dependency on welfare, the likelihood that the law will succeed at bringing lasting reform is doubtful.

One fact that is certain is that the poor have always been a part of every society. The problem is not that people are poor; it is how to help them become self-sufficient. Modern day welfare began as an effort to help poor children. Prior to this time, the poor had received charity in various forms, initially in their homes and then by being sent to institutions or workhouses. This early effort was known as Outdoor Relief and was later reformed by the Scientific Charity movement, which promoted the idea that individuals should work to earn charity, and if they were unable to work, they should be sent to institutions. The first formal welfare program began in 1915 in the state of Illinois, which broke with the conventions of Scientific Charity and began providing small pensions to widows and children. Following Illinois' lead, forty other states enacted their own pension programs, which were called "mother's pensions." After the Great Depression, the Social Security Act (SSA) of 1935 provided states that had pension payments with federal assistance to help relieve fiscal stress. With additional funding, states were able to expand the services they provided to these single mothers. The objective of the SSA was to encourage mothers to stay at home and rear their children instead of entering the job market (Morris and Thompson 4). Women were discouraged from becoming self-reliant by having their benefits reduced by one hundred percent of the value of their earnings if they took a job (Mills 14). While this kept women out of the workplace, it also helped to promote dependency on the welfare system. Unable to work because of the penalty of losing their benefits, these women became prisoners of the system. It is interesting to note that the original objective of the federal program has now become its biggest source of contention.

Welfare rolls continued to grow as the economy in this country changed. Hit by the recession, companies which were once major employers were unable to compete with local and foreign competitors and had to go out of business. The impact of these closings was that in some areas of the country, entire communities found themselves unemployed. If the business was the only major employer, smaller businesses also closed as people began to move to other cities to look for work. Companies that were able to stay in business had to lay off many of its employees in order to stay profitable. People who had received unemployment compensation after losing their job, then found themselves applying for welfare. As bad as conditions were in our country, they were better than the situations in other countries, so immigrants, both legal and illegal, continued to enter the country searching for a better life. Immigrants were blamed for taking jobs from American citizens, but immigrants usually worked in menial jobs that no one else would take. Some immigrants worked several jobs but were still unable to support their families and began applying for welfare benefits.

As the cost of providing welfare continued to rise, federal and state governments continued to pour money into the system. What was supposed to be a "helping hand" soon became a way of life for many recipients. Successful efforts at moving people from welfare into the workplace were the exception rather than the rule. Many recipients needed additional education and training before they would be able to enter the job market. Programs were created to provide this education, but as reports of fraudulent schools and inadequate training began to surface, public opinion about welfare began to push harder for reform. Confronted with stories of "welfare queens" who lived in luxury while defrauding the welfare system and multiple generations who received welfare, the public became less sympathetic towards welfare recipients. Recipients were now seen as deadbeats who were able but unwilling to work. They were no longer seen as victims of the poverty they lived in but as those who made the choice to stay on welfare because it was a free handout.

With this changing attitude and the need to reduce federal spending, reform continued to remain at the forefront of political debate. According to Elizabeth Sawhill of the Urban Institute, four prevailing issues of the welfare system exist:

- It does not provide sufficient state flexibility.
- It does not encourage work.
- It is responsible for the breakdown of the family, especially for the rising tide of out-of-wedlock births.
- It has done little to reduce poverty, especially among children. (1)

While these and other issues were major factors of reforming the welfare system, so was the need to reduce federal spending. The Federal Government paid 55% of all AFDC benefits to each state, regardless of the number of recipients (Poole 2). The Republican-controlled Congress had vowed to "balance the budget," and welfare spending was one of the areas where major cuts were proposed. In 1996, Congress passed H.R. 3734, also known as the Personal Responsibility and Work Opportunity Act of 1996, which was signed into law by President Clinton in August of the same year (H.R. 3734.1). People on both sides of the issue are speculating the impact the law will have. Proponents of the law believe that it will turn freeloading mothers into working, respectable citizens. Opponents of the law believe it will be increase the number of homeless people and that gangs of children will now roam the streets (Cottle 5). The provisions of the law that they believe will have the most negative impact are "Title I: Block Grants for Temporary Assistance for Needy Families (TANF); Title IV: Restricting Welfare and Public Benefits for Aliens; and Title VII: Food Stamps and Commodity Distribution" (H. R. 3734.1).

Title I of the law replaces Aid to Families with Dependent Children (AFDC) and Job Opportunities and Basic Skills Training (JOBS) programs with the Temporary Assistance for Needy Families (TANF). According to one source, States will receive fixed block grants for the next six years. The amount of the grant will be based upon previous AFDC spending levels (Zedlweski and Giannarelli 1). Unlike previous welfare provisions, the block grant will not increase as a State's caseload increases. It also requires that

> State TANF programs establish mandatory work requirements and provide education and job-related activities for the purpose of: (1) providing such families with time-limited assistance to end their dependency on government benefits and achieve self-sufficiency; (2) preventing and reducing out-of-wedlock pregnancies, especially teen ones; and (3) encouraging the formulation and maintenance of two-parent families. (H.R. 3734 2)

Not only will recipients have to find a job under TANF, but also they must do so within a specified time period. Recipients who are not employed after two years will receive reduced benefits; overall, families may receive TANF for no more than five years, and adults receiving assistance must find employment within three months, or their food stamps will be terminated (Poole 2). States may waive this requirement for 20% of their caseload[1] or they may request a waiver of the employment requirement if the state has a high unemployment rate.

Perhaps the most controversial section of the law is Title IV, which terminates all federal benefits to legal immigrants. Fix and Zimmerman comment that not only are immigrants ineligible for federal finds but also that state and local governments can choose to exclude immigrants from state and local assistance eligibility (2). It is hoped that the measure will not only reduce federal spending but also reduce the number of immigrants coming into the United States. The latter objective is probably the least likely to occur since the majority of people who migrate to this country are leaving conditions that are much worse than anything they would encounter here.

Although harsh measures had to be taken in order to reform welfare, implementing some of the measures will prove a challenge to many states. Michelle Cottle notes that administering welfare under the new law will mean increased workloads for agency caseworkers (9). Not only will they have to perform their previous duties of screening applicants and calculating benefits, they will also need to monitor and track the progress of applicants to make sure that they are in compliance with the guidelines (Cottle 9). At a time when many agencies are reducing their staff due to budget cuts, monitoring the new regulations will put increasing pressure on existing staff.

Moving people from welfare into the workforce is another requisite of the law that will be a challenge to implement. The law gives states one year to find jobs for 25% of their caseload, but many families who are long term and teenage recipients are unskilled and/or uneducated. These two groups, as well as others, will need education and training in order to enter the job market. The cost of providing this training will be the responsibility of individual states since the law provides no funding for these programs even though it requires that states offer training and job assistance. After completion of the required training, the next obstacle for recipients will be finding work. Even with additional training, many recipients will only qualify for minimum wage positions, which will not help them rise above the poverty level. With the U.S. economy currently experiencing a low unemployment rate, available jobs will probably require advanced job skills, training, and knowledge. Welfare recipients trying to enter the job market will be competing against non-recipients who will be more educated and have more work experience.

Immigrants in this country will be the first to feel the impact of the new reform. One can only imagine the hardship that current immigrants will experience because of the termination of their eligibility. While writers of the law envision that disqualifying immigrants will help reduce the federal deficit and curtail immigration to this country, they overlooked the human toll this provision will cause. Fix and Zimmerman estimate that 569,000 recipients (three-fourths) will lose their benefits immediately; 252,000[2] families will receive reduced benefits and 520,000 (three-fourths) SSI recipients would lose their benefits (2). States may choose whether or not to deny state assistance to immigrants, but either choice will have adverse effects. If states extend assistance to immigrants, then they are responsible for the full cost of any assistance. If states deny assistance, a substantial segment of their population will be left without any resources. In states with large immigrant populations, this could have dire consequences.

Samuel Taylor Coleridge said, "Every reform, however necessary will . . . be carried to an excess, that itself will need reforming" (qtd. in Poole 1). The problem of reforming the welfare system is that for many years it was easier for government to continue to put money into the program rather than search for long-term solutions that would enable people to move from the welfare rolls into the job market with the training and skills necessary to be competitive. It was evident that the welfare system had become inadequate long before the Clinton administration, but neither Congress nor previous presidents were able to agree on a plan to change the welfare system. In the midst of a budget crisis with the deficit continuing to rise, the government has had to reduce or cut many programs. In reducing spending on welfare, I believe that tough guidelines had to be established, but some of the provisions of the law go beyond motivating people into the job market. The law seeks to move literally hundreds of thousands of individuals off the welfare rolls into the job market; however, many recipients will be unable to compete in a job market that requires a minimum of a bachelor's degree for positions. With the loss of federal benefits after five years, people who are still unable to find work will look to state and local agencies for additional support. Many states are writing their own welfare reform that would also set a maximum period for receiving benefits. We can only speculate at the repercussions to individuals who have no means of supporting themselves. The mandates of the new law are intended to reduce the federal budget and create productive citizens from former welfare recipients. While this is a good intention, studies indicate that it will require additional money in order for the provisions to be successful (Poole 2). Although the Personal Responsibility and Work Opportunity Act of 1996 was enacted to discourage and eliminate dependency on welfare, the likelihood that the law will succeed at bringing long-term reform is doubtful.

Notes

1. Those eligible for exclusion are mothers with children under six.

2. Typically these families will be made up of immigrant parents with children who are U. S. citizens. The children will still be eligible to receive benefits but their parents will not be.

Works Cited

Cottle, Michelle. "Reforming Welfare Reform". Washington Monthly, Nov 1996: 9-15. Periodical Abstracts. Online. 20 Feb 1997.

Fix, Michael, and Wendy Zimmerman. "When Should Immigrants Receive Public Benefits?" Welfare Reform: An Analysis of the Issues. Ed. Isabel V. Sawhill. The Urban Institute. America Online. Internet. 12 Feb 1997. Available http://www.urban.org/welfare/chap15.htm.

Mills, Frederick B. "The Ideology of Welfare Reform: Deconstructing Stigma." Social Work 41.4. (Jul 1996): 391-395. Periodical Abstracts. Online. 20 Feb. 1997.

Norris, Donald F., and Lyke Thompson, eds. The Politics of Welfare Reform. Thousand Oaks: Sage, 1995.

Poole, Dennis L. "Welfare Reform: The Bad, the Ugly, and the Maybe not too Awful." Health and Social Work 21.4. (Nov 1996): 243-246. Periodical Abstracts. Online. 20 Feb 1997.

Sawhill, Isabel V., ed. Welfare Reform: An Analysis of the Issues. The Urban Institute. America Online. Internet. 12 Feb.1997. Available http://www.urban.org/welfare/overview.htm.

United States. Congress. House. Personal Responsibility and Work Opportunity Reconciliation Act of 1996. 104th Congress, H.R. 3734. America Online. Internet. 24 Feb 1997. Available http://thomas.loc.gov/cgi-bin/bdquery/z?d104:HR03734:@@@D.

Zedlewski, Sheila, and Linda Giannarelli. "Diversity Among State Welfare Programs: Implications for Reform." New Federalism: Issues and Options for States (Series No. A-i). Wash, D.C., The Urban Institute, Jan 1997.1-8.

The Influence of Fate in "Swaddling Clothes" & "A Woman like Me"

Manuela Saramondi

ENSL 016/Literary Analysis, Primary Source

Fate is what is going to happen that is not under human control. In the two stories "Swaddling Clothes" and "A Woman like Me," both main characters believe in fate even though they face it differently.

In "Swaddling Clothes" by Mishima Yukio, the main character of Toshiko is described as an oversensitive, timid, and non-adventurous person. As a result of constant worrying, she never put on weight, and now as an adult woman, she looks "more like a transparent picture than a creature of flesh and blood" (132). Because of her sensitivity toward the injustices of destiny, she finds herself feeling somewhat responsible for the maid's baby who is born in her house. This baby, who is born out of wedlock and wrapped in newspaper instead of proper swaddling clothes, will be a victim of the world's stereotyping: "Toshiko, whose own life has been spent in solid comfort, poignantly feels the wretchedness of the illegitimate baby" (133). The destiny of the baby is already planned. He is going to have a miserable life, similar to how he had a miserable birth. Toshiko is the only one who sees that scene; therefore, she feels responsible for the child's future, but especially for her own child's destiny. She wants to prevent fate from ruining her son's life in the future: "One day by a quirk of fate, he meets the other boy, who then will also have turned twenty. And say that the other boy, who has been sinned against, savagely stabs him with a knife . . . " (134). She is worried about what could happen, so her belief in fate takes her to search for some kind of sign that will help her to change the course of destiny.

She finds the sign in the park where she sees a homeless man wrapped with newspaper: "Her fear and premonitions have suddenly taken concrete form" (136). The newspaper used as a cover for him and for society is the symbol of misery and insecurity. It is the fear present in her premonitions, so she is ready to face destiny. Toshiko sacrifices herself to the course of events so that her son will not have to have any encounters with her premonitions. She tries to make swaddling clothes of security for her son.

In "A Woman like Me" by Xi Xi, the main character, who is a cosmetologist for dead bodies, is described as an uncommunicative, honest, and brave person. She is also described as a paler and natural looking girl: "Both my hands and my face are paler than most people because of my job" (153). Consequently, she is stereotyped by society's fear. Her job is the cause of her solitude. Nobody wants to be around someone who works with dead people. She is doing this job not because she likes it, but because she believes it is her destiny. Her aunt taught this belief to her, and she believes that both have the same destiny: "I am totally powerless to resist fate, which has played a cruel trick on me" (152). The trick is her inability to fight fate and, therefore, her inability to change her destiny.

Even though the main character has a lot of good qualities, no man will accept her profession. Her job and her honesty make her live an isolated life. Her job makes her uncommunicative because no dialogue can be held with the dead and also because she doesn't want to reveal her profession. She prefers to live on assumptions, especially now that she has a boyfriend that she loves and she doesn't want to lose him. She knows he will probably leave her when he finds out about her job: "A woman like me is actually unsuitable for any man's love" (162). She is not fighting for her happiness; she is blindly accepting her destiny. An example of her weakness in facing fate is when she refuses to perform her job on a couple that committed suicide: "I know that, considering my position, I should have nothing to do with anyone who lacked the courage to resist the forces of fate" (157). She is not timid toward dead people, but she is very timid toward fate. She has faith in fate, and she expects people to have faith in love: "Why do people who are falling in love have so little faith in love? Why do they not have courage in their love?" (158). She blames people and herself for being so weak toward something that is not possible to control. She has courage in her faith, but people don't have courage in their love. She sacrifices her happiness for her belief in fate, and then she challenges her fate for her momentary happiness.

Fate, in both stories, is the conflict which both characters have to deal with. Their lives are connected with fate, but while Toshika in "Swaddling Clothes" finds a way to change her destiny, the central character in "A Woman like Me" passively accepts the course of her destiny. Toshiko wants to create security for her son in this world, while the lady in "A Woman like Me" wants to create security for herself in the other world.

◆◆◆

Both stories can be found in the following text:

Spack, Ruth, ed. The International Story: An Anthology with Guidelines for Reading and Writing about Fiction. New York: St. Martin's, 1994.

A Father's Influence in *Washington Square*

Lois Jones

English 1102/Literary Analysis, Primary Source

Psychological damage to children often occurs as a result of excessive disapproval and lack of parental love. In extreme cases, this treatment can affect the personal growth in children and may be irreversible as they approach adulthood. Catherine Sloper, in Henry James's Washington Square, like many children, was mentally affected by these factors. She had a father who did not love her, who doubted any suitor could find her desirable, and who manipulated her to accomplish his desires. These three perceptions account for the father's negative impact on Catherine.

First, we must understand the true feelings Dr. Sloper had for his daughter. Dr. Sloper had loved his wife very much because she was beautiful and brilliant. However, she died a few days after Catherine's birth. Dr. Sloper was a well-respected and intelligent doctor in the community; therefore, he was obligated to meet his parental responsibility. Outwardly to the community, he met his fatherly commitments; however, he began the mental damage to Catherine by immediately comparing her to her mother. In his mind, Catherine did not measure up. Dr. Sloper even made comments to Elizabeth, Catherine's aunt, concerning Catherine's lack of beauty during a discussion of her marriageable future: "They [bachelors] prefer pretty girls -- lively girls -- girls like your own. Catherine is neither pretty nor lively," Dr. Sloper commented (35). Catherine also disappointed him because she was not brilliant in her classes, and he told Catherine's aunt to make her clever. Dr. Sloper's opinion was that if Catherine was unattractive, maybe she could at least be clever.

It is only natural to assume that if Dr. Sloper makes these comments to others, his behavior and treatment of Catherine would demonstrate his beliefs to her. This subconscious knowledge would only increase these perceived weaknesses; Catherine had no reason to doubt her intelligent and respected father. Studies have been conducted on children that show they become what parents expect of them. Because Dr. Sloper saw Catherine as simple, big and unattractive, Catherine lived up to his expectations. She overate--probably due to her own insecurities--had difficulty in expressing herself, and could not excel in anything. There are references made to the purchase of cream cakes (8), inability to express her feelings to Morris (20), and her inability to excel at school or music (8-9).

Another powerful display of how little Dr. Sloper loved his daughter was the manner in which he handled her first love. When Morris Townsend began to pursue Catherine, her father immediately sized up the situation and determined that he was after her money. Dr. Sloper, having come to this conclusion, then decided that Catherine could not marry Morris. This decision was based on Dr. Sloper's dislike for lazy, worthless people rather than any concern for his daughter's welfare (40). If he had loved his daughter, he would have been concerned about her getting hurt and handled the situation more delicately. Instead, he told Catherine that Morris was just after the money. Once again this confirmed for Catherine, now in young adulthood, her simple and undesireable traits.

At this point (47), Dr. Sloper began his experimental manipulation of Catherine to confirm his own intelligence. Knowing how Catherine felt about him and Morris, he forced her to choose between them so he could observe the struggle. At one point Dr. Sloper shows his enjoyment of the manipulation by saying the following: "I believe she will stick -- I believe she will stick!" (101). And this idea of Catherine "sticking" appeared to have a comical side to Dr. Sloper and to offer a prospect of entertainment.

To further manipulate the outcome, Dr. Sloper told both Morris and Catherine that if they married, she would not get an inheritance. He knew Morris would not persuade Catherine to marry him without the money, and this would prove Dr. Sloper was right about him. This proof of his superiority was what Dr. Sloper desired more than he cared about the feelings of his daughter (184). The last move in Dr. Sloper's manipulation game and evidence of his total disregard for his daughter was the denial of her inheritance upon his death.

Based on all of these factors, Dr. Sloper was clearly responsible for the demise of Catherine. No child should ever have to endure such an unloving environment. Although Dr. Sloper did not physically abuse his daughter, he mentally abused her. He did not verbally tell her that he did not love her, nor did he tell her that she was unattractive and unintelligent. However, each day of Catherine's life, her father's actions demonstrated these facts. It was not until adulthood that Catherine realized her father did not love her (141-2). By this time, so much mental damage had been done that it was not possible for Catherine to see her father for what he was and to regain a new appreciation for herself. Catherine was so crippled by the years of her father's treatment she had withdrawn into a world of worthlessness.

James, Henry. Washington Square. 1880. Ed. Mark Le Fanu. Oxford: Oxford UP, 1982.

Why the Caged Bird Sings

Zahra McAllister

English 1102/Literary Analysis, Primary Source

Dunbar's poem "Sympathy" holds a myriad of symbols. Literally, the speaker empathizes with a caged bird that sings out of sadness and loneliness. Clearly, the bird's sorrow comes from being imprisoned and alone in a cage. The symbolic message, however, is much harder to grasp. African-Americans of Dunbar's time, like the caged bird, were trapped in symbolic cages and even sometimes treated as beautiful show pieces. Dunbar uses a caged bird as a symbol of the African-Americans' reaction to being isolated, held captive, and considered unequal.

Like a caged bird, African-Americans a hundred years ago were socially isolated. While strong "literal" bars caged the bird, the chains of racism were equally as confining to African-Americans. Similar to the bird, the people could see the beauty of the outside world, but they could never be a part of the splendor. Through the bars of their cages, they saw a life of freedom, but they found the chains of racism too strong to escape. By being caged, the people were being raped in the sense that their culture was violated and their bodies were shoved into a place where they could never be free as a bird which can only "fly back to his perch and cling" (line 10). African-Americans clung to the life they knew and waited for the day when they could experience the beauty of freedom.

The bird, like the African-American people, was held captive but was inspired by the longing to be free. In his attempt to be free, the bird fought and mutilated himself to no avail. Similar to the bird, the African- Americans fought to escape the cruelty of being caged in by racism. The people shed blood to be released from the captivity of their symbolic cages. In his quest for freedom, the bird "beat his wing / Till its blood is red on the cruel bars" (lines 8-9). Likewise, the people were distraught to find their struggles in vain and their wings useless; the bars of injustice were too confining. Finally, with bruised wings and throbbing hearts, the people continued to beat their "cages" in a seemingly useless attempt to gain freedom. After the endless struggle, they could only plead and pray because their hearts were too heavy to do much more.

African-Americans, like the bird, were caged by inequality. While a cage was the bird's prison, the people were enslaved by injustice. The bird and the people sang of not only sadness but also of being caged by racism. Literal bars held the bird in his cage, but the symbolic bars of racism kept African-Americans from being equal. The music sung by the people and the bird sounded beautiful and was mistaken for a "carol of joy or glee" (line 18). In reality, the songs were used to mask the internal scars formed by inequality.

"I know what the caged bird feels, alas!" (line 1)--the speaker feels pain from being isolated, held captive, and considered unequal. Like the caged bird, African-Americans longed to be free. The prisoners did not sing out of happiness, but they let their songs ring out as a prayer for justice. Although people were hurt and bruised, they continued to hope and pray for deliverance. The bird, like the people, was strong, yet bewildered. He understood that while he might never be released, his struggles, prayers, and pleas might bring freedom to his children.

The Endurance of Our Foremothers

Coretia Rutledge

English 1102/Literary Analysis
with Secondary Source

Myth has it that we live similar lives to those of our parents, but in her poem "Lineage," Margaret Walker questions the similarity of her life to her grandmothers'. She writes of her grandmothers' strength as they struggled with life in the South during the antebellum period. She was inspired by the stories often told to her by her grandmother. She took these stories and structured her own writing around telling the stories that her grandmothers had told her long ago.

In her essay "How I Wrote *Jubilee,*" Margaret Walker explains how her continuous curiosity that was created from her grandmothers' stories controlled her life. She writes, "Since my grandmother lived with us until I was an adult, it was natural throughout my formative years for me to hear stories of life in Georgia" (51). The aspects of her grandmothers' lives that struck her curiosity were the realities that they were able to overcome, such as the abuse and struggles of the severe era in the South. Her grandmothers filled her soul with stories of the lives of the men and women who struggled so that those who were to come after them would have the opportunity to live better lives. Closely parallel to the lives of her grandmothers as her poem is, she writes:

> My grandmothers are full of memories
> Smelling of soap and onions and wet clay
> With veins running roughly over quick hands
> They have many clean words to say. (lines 7-10)

The lives of her grandmothers were truly full of memories that they kept with them until their dying days. Their memories were also carried along by their children and their children's children. She also speaks of the pain that was revealed to her through her grandmothers' hands. With age, their hands continue to show the hardships that they survived.

Walker admired the strength of her foremothers. She expressed her admiration in her poem when she speaks of the work they did by saying,

> They touched the earth and grain grew.
> They were full of sturdiness and singing
> My grandmothers were strong. (lines 4-6)

The poem reveals that although her grandmothers had to struggle, they strove to keep going. Although these women worked so strenuously, never did they hang their heads or want to give up their fight. They were driven by their strength and the power of song. She goes on to speak of the power that her grandmothers had of touching the earth and being able to produce. The many stories that her grandmothers told her were filled with aspiration and life. Margaret Walker states, "Most of my life I have been involved with writing this story about my great-grandmother "(50). Her deep gratitude to her grandmothers made her want to share with the world how they helped to make her life a little easier.

In the last stanza of her poem, Margaret Walker questions, "Why am I not as they" (line 12). Her grandmothers struggled for her, and she accomplished many tasks because of the advantages acquired from their struggle. Therefore, she centered her life around educating others about the knowledge of their past. She made a path for her family to follow just as her grandmothers did for her. Yet she still questions the worth of her life in comparison to the accomplishments of her grandmothers. Their struggles allowed her to become educated, and her interest in education led her to teach others. Margaret Walker has several things in her life that she should acknowledge as her grandmothers' legacy. Hers was a different struggle from her grandmothers', but all the same it was a struggle. She acquired freedom and endurance from her grandmothers and, in turn, was able to fight for civil rights and provide her children with an education.

◆◆◆

Works Cited

Walker, Margaret. "How I Wrote *Jubilee*" and Other Essays. New York: Feminist Press, 1990.

---. "Lineage." Literature. 3rd ed. Ed. Robert DiYanni. New York: McGraw, 1994. 690.

◆◆◆

"The difference between the right word
and the almost right word
is the difference between lightning and the
lightning bug."

Mark Twain

In 1996, The Chattahoochee Review devoted its fall issue to a *festschrift* celebrating the life and works of one of the South's and the nation's finest fiction writers, Madison Percy Jones. Mr. Jones was invited to DeKalb for the presentation of the issue and while here made appearances on the Dunwoody and Lawrenceville campuses where he lectured, read from his works, and conversed with students. The students enjoyed their time with Mr. Jones. Several of them set up a web-site about him on the Internet, while others in various English 102 classes wrote their literary research papers on topics related to his 1989 novel Last Things (L.S.U. Press). Many excellent papers were written; two of the finest appear in the following pages.

Hawthorne and Jones: The Legacy Lives On

Nancy Baumgarten

English 1102/Literary Analysis, Researched

To withstand the test of time is one of the greatest accomplishments any writer can hope to achieve. There is no better indication of such a success than by creating a work of art which later serves as an influence on another artist. Such is the case with Nathaniel Hawthorne's short story "Young Goodman Brown," written in the nineteenth century, and Madison Jones's Last Things, a twentieth-century novel. Jones has even directly stated, in an interview with Carl Griffin, that he "was much influenced by Hawthorne" ("Conversation" 123). Furthermore, Wilson Hall, a former student of Jones at Auburn University, recalls that Jones used Hawthorne's "Young Goodman Brown" as an example of how to "create a rich enlacement of themes, ideas, and symbols which lift the whole to an art form of complexity and beauty reserved usually for music" (29). Although there are some differences between Hawthorne's "Young Goodman Brown" and Jones's Last Things, the two narratives are amazingly similar in many respects, revealing the influence of Hawthorne's story on Jones's novel. These influences are seen in the authors' presentation of tone, the psychomachic development of the protagonists, and the major theme of evil in both works.

The main difference between "Young Goodman Brown" and Last Things lies in what protagonists have become at the end of the narratives. Young Goodman Brown, as a solid citizen of the Puritan community descended from "a race of honest men and good Christians" (Hawthorne 151), seems spiritually destroyed by his possible nocturnal encounter with the Evil One in the forest at night: "A stern, a sad, a darkly meditative, a distrustful, if not a desperate man did he become from the night of that fearful dream" (163). Leo B. Levy, in his essay "The Problem of Faith in 'Young Goodman Brown,'" has noted that at the end of the narrative, Brown has "irrevocably fallen into gloom and despair, condemned to live a long life of withdrawal and suspicion" (118). He can no longer bear to listen to his minister and congregation pray, and he even grows distant from his wife Faith. Overall, his experience has made him an isolated, lonely, and cynical man whose "dying hour was gloom" (Hawthorne 163). Hawthorne suggests that because Brown has gone out on a journey in search of evil, he finds it, and in a sense sees without his "Faith" a projection of his own evil, a spiritually destructive revelation.

On the other hand, Wendell Corbin seems restored by his possible encounter with true evil. He has evolved from a lonely, unemotional man to one with compassion as he is moving towards a more spiritual view of the world. By the end of the novel, he seems to have moved away from the nihilistic views of Nietzsche to the more open-minded views of Kant. Wendell is finally caring for people for the first time, as shown by the close relationship he develops with Preacher Sears and the moving final scene with his father. Edwin T. Arnold has noted that while Jones "believes strongly in the existence of sin and the inevitability of retribution, [he] also sees the possibility of redemption" (1487). Thus, at the end of the novel, Jones presents Wendell, with "gratitude welling up in him" (<u>L.T.</u> 206), on the verge of full redemption. Jones suggests that because Wendell's encounter with evil was "something fated to be" (<u>L.T.</u> 1), and not something he planned and went in search of like Young Goodman Brown, he is perhaps able to overcome his experience. The clear contrast between the defeated Young Goodman Brown and the restored Wendell Corbin serves as the major difference between the two literary works.

Despite this difference, the two works prove to be incredibly alike, showing the influence of the story on the development of the novel. Their similarity is first revealed by an examination of the narratives' tones. In this discussion, rather than Mr. I. A. Richards' definition of tone as an attitude, the definition of Brooks and Warren emphasizing atmosphere will be employed. They define tone as "the organizing intelligence of the work--the spirit of a work . . . " (310). In "Young Goodman Brown," a sense of impending doom and despair pervades the entire short story. Brian Harding, a Senior Lecturer in the English Department of the University of Birmingham, appropriately comments that there is "no uncertainty of tone in 'Young Goodman Brown' . . .[the short story is] sombre throughout" (x). As Brown journeys into the forest plagued with insecurity about his decision, he takes "a dreary road, darkened by all of the gloomiest trees of the forest" (Hawthorne 150). This road, coupled with "frightful sounds--the creaking of trees, the howling of wild beasts, and the yell of Indians" (157), adds to the fearful atmosphere that emerges. There is, furthermore, the sense of being followed throughout the story as Goodman Brown feels there "may be a devilish Indian behind every tree" (150). With such an ominous world portrayed, Brown is completely destroyed by his encounter with evil, and the narrative appropriately ends with "no hopeful verse" (163) written upon his tombstone.

Similarly, Last Things is primarily dominated by this same tone. As Jones satirizes the modern academic world, the novel begins in a humorous way. But once Wendell is set up by Cat Bird, the humor vanishes and is replaced entirely by feelings of desperation and doom. Joanne Childers notes this change of tone, that the novel "initially promises to be humorous in its portrayals of the groves of academe. Inevitably, however, evil enters the story, humor fails, and the characters act out the moral tale" (17). Meetings with Jason Farrow, who could possibly be the Devil himself, are always held at night, in a "curtain of darkness" (Jones, L.T. 98), with the eerie sounds of screech owls to emphasize the gloom. In addition, these meetings involve the staircase that Wendell must climb in order to reach Farrow, possibly suggesting the Devil's exalted position, and also emphasizing Wendell's deeper descent into the world of evil with every ascending step. As Wendell becomes more and more involved with the drug world, fear and despair dominate the tone as the reader realizes that Wendell is "afloat face-down at the bottom of a dark hole" (L.T. 64). There is also the constant sense of a "figure that [stands] there watching--watching Wendell" (L.T. 15). Carl Griffin also notices that most characters in Jones's novels feel as if they are "being pursued . . . . They often feel that they are not only being stared at by invisible presences but are actually being followed and chased" (Jones, "Conv." 131), much as Wendell does throughout Last Things. Thus, the ominous and desperate tone of the two works serves as a definite similarity between them and indicates a more than probable influence of Hawthorne on Jones.

A second similarity between the narratives lies in the psychomachic development of the protagonists as they both feel themselves drawn between the forces of good and evil. As Young Goodman Brown journeys into the forest at night, Richard P. Adams notices that he meets the Devil, who tries to persuade him to attend the witches' meeting, thus personifying the evil force attempting to draw Brown deeper into the forest (164). This second traveler, who represents the Devil himself and who carries a staff which seems to be a black snake, complains that Brown is late and urges him to speed up his "dull pace for the beginning of a journey" (Hawthorne 151). As the short story opens, it is "Faith [which] kept [Brown] back a while" (150), seemingly representing the forces of good, but she, too, will appear at the sabbath, in Brown's view, that night. Therefore, the only remaining forces of good for Brown are his mother, "a woman, with dim features of despair" (160), who tries to reach out to her son and save him from the Devil, and Brown's conscience as he thinks "what a wretch I am to leave [my wife] on such an errand" (150). Richard H. Fogle explains that the night in the forest falls naturally into two parts: the temptation by the Devil and the resistance by Brown's conscience. Fogle also notices Brown's struggle as he is "half-eager and half-reluctant" to make his journey (28). Drawn by his mother and conscience on one side and the Devil on the other, the struggle is indeed a difficult one, and Brown even feels that he has "no power to retreat one step, nor to resist" (Hawthorne 160).

Likewise, Wendell Corbin finds himself, like "a goat on a rope" (Jones, L.T. 64), pulled between the forces of good and evil and believes that "his soul [has] been the object of some discarnate form of manipulation" (187). Daphne Day, in her book review of Last Things, notices this psychomachic struggle that Wendell undergoes as he "enters into a state of intense mental and emotional turmoil" (195). Carl Griffin, likewise, realizes that this struggle is common to most of Jones's characters, as they all seem to go through this struggle of the mind and spirit (Jones, "Conv." 130). Drawn into the clutches of the toad-like Jason Farrow, who is the embodiment of true evil and possibly the Devil himself, Wendell discovers that he is up against a powerful source capable of destruction as he hears of Venutti's tragic murder. First set up and then lured in by the prospect of becoming "a rich Corbin" (Jones, L.T. 79), Wendell experiences this evil as apparent and strong. Cat Bird, an extension of the evil Farrow, also seems to pull Wendell in the direction of the drug world, and even before this present summer Wendell was "almost as glad to be getting rid of Cat as of anything else" (34) when he had left Bliss County for college some years earlier.

Preacher Sears, representing the force of good, is the embodiment of everything that lies in opposition to Farrow and Cat Bird. Even the very first time Wendell sees Sears from a distance, he seem to possess an almost magnetlike pull on the boy as Wendell stops to watch this towering figure and even experiences "what felt like conscience in him" (81). He serves as the key to salvation for Wendell at the end of the novel as he takes care of Wendell in the hope of "saving another soul" (203.) His ally, Mrs. Harker, who used to help Sears financially when he was a young child, has an apparent supernatural hold over Wendell's mind and also emerges as a force of good and a representation of the old order of society as she attempts to expose Farrow's participation in the drug world.

Luckily, in the struggle for Wendell's soul, the forces of good are stronger than those of evil. As Jones presents Wendell in the pyschomachic struggle, he "demonstrates that it is almost impossible for an individual to exist apart from a social framework," especially in the struggle for his soul (Gretlund 115). It is indeed apparent that both Young Goodman Brown and Wendell Corbin undergo a similar kind of psychomachic struggle, revealing yet another influence of Hawthorne's story on Jones's novel.

Finally, the main theme of both works illustrates a major similarity between them. Both narratives explore the question of whether metaphysical evil has an objective essence or merely lies in the minds of men. F. O. Matthiessen notes that Hawthorne's conception of evil can be accounted for by his background, particularly his relation to a "phase of decay of the Puritan tradition" (186). It is this view of evil that Hawthorne explores as the major theme of his short story. In "Young Goodman Brown," much evidence is presented to suggest to the reader that Brown's journey into the forest is indeed a real one. In addition, the second traveler with Brown, who carries the snakelike staff and seems to look like his father, is possibly the Devil. Thus, the short story suggests the objective existence of evil in the world. However, while presenting this notion, Nathaniel Hawthorne simultaneously leaves the question open in the minds of his readers by asking, "Had Goodman Brown fallen asleep in the forest and only dreamed a wild dream of a witch-meeting?" (162). Furthermore, the next morning, Hawthorne has Brown discover that "a hanging twig, that had been all on fire [in his dream], besprinkled his cheek with the coldest dew" (162), again suggesting the notion that all of the night's events took place in Brown's mind. Arlin Turner states that Hawthorne believed his presentation of material would be better "if he raised questions, suggested alternative answers, and left the reader to formulate his own conclusions" (131). Hawthorne, therefore, employs equivocation and ambiguity from beginning to end, and he leaves many questions unanswered. What he does state emphatically, however, is the profound effect the experience in the forest, whether real or imagined, has had on the protagonist of the story.

In much the same manner, Jones presents in Last Things this same theme of whether or not cosmic evil truly exists. Jan N. Gretlund realizes that addressing evil as a main theme is not a new routine for Jones, as most of his works seem to revolve around some force of evil (109). As Hawthorne's view of evil is based on a Puritan background, Jones has stated that the common theme of evil in his work is based upon a similar "Puritanical sense of evil and wrongdoing" ("Conv." 123) but within a

Southern setting. Believing that evil is "an abiding, active force" (Hoffman 81), Jones seems to be presenting the objective existence of evil in the world as he describes Wendell Corbin's contact with Jason Farrow and his descent into the drug world in completely believable and realistic terms. Wendell has conversations with real people and describes his trips to bribe officers and help with the airship operations realistically and with much specification.

As the novel comes to a close, however, Jones creates doubt in the mind of the reader as he has Wendell wonder whether all of his summer activities have been "something interrupted--or [were] they only imagined?" (L.T. 175). In addition, Wendell comes to believe that people "know very little about objective reality and the part of it [they] do perceive is not only a mere fraction of the whole but a fraction interpreted or pictured according to the structure of [their] mental faculties" (176). The reader is given two options in the novel—to believe that the evil is real and exists or is merely imagined by Wendell in his mind, which is often altered by drugs. Jones does show how the psychiatrists and detectives fail to believe Wendell's story of his summer experiences. He also proves Wendell's ability to hallucinate, especially when he has an entirely imaginary conversation with Preacher Sears in his home after Mrs. Harker's death, since it is later revealed that Sears had no knowledge of where Wendell lived. But these pieces of evidence still do not entirely prove that the remaining action of the novel also lies exclusively within the mind of Wendell. Jones states that in Last Things, the "ambiguity is deliberate," and Carl Griffin has responded by indicating that the fact that the "reader is not sure how much is really true" is a major strength of the novel (Jones, "Conv." 123). What is clear is that both Hawthorne and Jones explore the major theme of whether Satanic evil exists or not and leave the ultimate decision up to the reader, with evidence pointing in both directions.

The themes of both works, furthermore, explore the extensiveness of evil in the world if it does, in fact, exist. In "Young Goodman Brown," perhaps what is most devastating to the protagonist is the overwhelming and comprehensive nature of sin. Robert P. Ellis notes how "literally everyone noted for sanctity seems to be gathered together in communion with known sinners before a rock altar amid blazing pine tress" (2737). Upon learning that Deacon Goodkin and the minister are involved in the evil gatherings and crimes of the village, Brown is "faint and overburdened with the heavy sickness of his heart" (Hawthorne 156). He furthermore comes to learn that his entire family, whom he thought were good Christian men, have been sinners, as is his catechizer Goody Cloyse. But the last straw for Brown comes when his precious wife, Faith, also seems to join the evil world. Overwhelmed by the apparent hypocrisy of his village and by the ubiquitous nature of evil in his world, he dies a lonely and depressed man with words of the Satanic minister of the witches' sabbath burned in his memory:

> Depending upon one another's heart, ye had still hoped that virtue were not all a dream. Now are ye undeceived. Evil is the nature of mankind. Evil must be your only happiness. Welcome again, my children, to the communion of your race. (161)

Jones, too, paints evil as an extremely overwhelming force if it truly exists. Daphne Day feels that the entire human world in the novel is "bleak [in that] relationships are barren, intellectuals are phonies, policemen are corrupt, [and] nearly everyone is on drugs" (196). Wendell is amazed to discover that "a fine man like Mr. Farrow" (Jones, L.T. 189), head of a car agency and a pillar of the community, could be involved in such an illegal and evil underworld. In addition, even the protectors of society are criminally involved, as a guilty Wendell correctly notes when he sees a police car: "He remembered: they were his cohorts, therefore friends" (155). The entire academic world is also part of the drug world, as Rathbone often has his "pot group" (12) parties, but this does not come as a surprise to Wendell. While Preacher Sears and Mrs. Harker are not taken in by the evil in society, it is clear that Jones is saying that if evil exists, it certainly is extensive. It is also significant that Jones has Mrs. Harker claim that she thinks "it's the devil who is in charge now" (101). Lee Smith makes it clear that "Jones is not afraid to tackle the great themes [and the fact that] this is a universe where evil exists, and actions have consequences" (90). In his novel, Jones would appear, then, to have taken under consideration a similar Puritan theme examined by his New England predecessor over a century earlier. How amazing it is that their conclusions and treatments of this theme so closely coincide.

The evidence from a close reading of Nathaniel Hawthorne's "Young Goodman Brown" and Madison Jones's Last Things is conclusive that there are astonishing similarities between the works on several levels and that the story obviously influenced the novel, as Jones himself has suggested ("Conv." 124). The question of influences between authors remains a literary mystery, much easier to cite than to explain. But such influences, in their inexplicable way, do exist. While Hawthorne's works, on their own merits, are masterpieces, "that significant later writers have found it important and even necessary to do similar things is the fullest tribute to the enduring quality of his achievement" (Martin 180). Madison Jones has helped indirectly to preserve Hawthorne's work, while at the same time creating a whole legacy of his own. And it may not be long before a future writer reaches back into Jones's novel for example and inspiration, for as Larry Brown, a new Southern writer, says:

> People like Madison Jones [are looked] up to the most, the ones who inspire [others] to try to carry on the great tradition that lives among Southern writers, both past and present, ever evolving and changing, but always owing so much to what has come before. (36)

Thus, the Jones-Hawthorne connection provides an example, illustrating how literary figures of each generation stand upon the shoulders of their predecessors to provide possible inspirational and artistic support for future masterpieces.

Works Cited

Adams, Richard P. "Hawthorne's Provincial Tales." New England Quarterly 30.1(1957): 39-57. Rpt. in "Nathaniel Hawthorne: 1804-1864." Short Story Criticism. Ed. Sheila Fitzgerald. Detroit: Gale, 1989. 163-168.

Arnold, Edwin T. "Madison Jones." Critical Survey of Long Fiction. Ed. Frank N. Magill. Englewood Cliffs: Salem, 1983. 1485-1495.

Brooks, Cleanth, and Robert Penn Warren. Modern Rhetoric: Shorter Edition. New York: Harcourt, 1961.

Brown, Larry. "Chattanooga Nights." The Chattahoochee Review 17.1 (1996): 33-37.

Childers, Joanne McEvilley. "Madison Jones—Place/ Person: The Effect of His Early Years on His Work." The Chattahoochee Review 17.1 (1996): 13-17.

Day, Daphne. Rev. of Last Things. Southern Humanities Review 25 (1991): 194-196.

Ellis, Robert P. "Young Goodman Brown." Masterplots II: Short Story Series. Ed. Frank N. Magill. Pasadena: Salem, 1986. 2737-2740.

Fogle, Richard H. "Young Goodman Brown." Hawthorne's Fiction: The Light and the Dark. Norman: U of Oklahoma P, 1952. 15-32.

Gretlund, Jan N. "The Mosses of an Old Tree: Madison Jones's *To the Winds.*" The Chattahoochee Review 17.1 (1996): 103-115.

Hall, Wilson. "A Memory of Madison Jones: Teacher." The Chattahoochee Review 17.1 (1996): 27-32.

Harding, Brian. "Introduction." Nathaniel Hawthorne. New York: Oxford UP, 1987. vii-xxxvi.

Hawthorne, Nathaniel. "Young Goodman Brown." Selected Tales and Sketches. Intro. Hyatt Waggoner. New York: Holt, 1970. 149-163.

Hoffman, William. "The Tempter Is Always with Us." The Chattahoochee Review 17.1 (1996): 74-81.

Jones, Madison P. Last Things. Baton Rouge: Louisiana State UP, 1989.

Jones, Madison P., and Carl Griffin. "Somewhere Outside of Auburn, Alabama: A Conversation with Madison Jones." The Chattahoochee Review 17.1 (1996): 116-137.

Levy, Leo B. "The Problem of Faith in 'Young Goodman Brown.'" Nathaniel Hawthorne. Ed. Harold Bloom. New York: Chelsea House, 1986. 115-126.

Martin, Terence. "A Significant Legacy." Nathaniel Hawthorne. Ed. Sylvia E. Bowen. New York: Twayne, 1965. 177-180.

Matthiessen, F. O. "Hawthorne's Psychology: The Acceptance of Good and Evil." The Recognition of Nathaniel Hawthorne. Ed. B. Bernard Cohen. Ann Arbor: U of Michigan P, 1969. 185-199.

Smith, Lee. "On Madison Jones." The Chattahoochee Review 17.1 (1996): 90.

Turner, Arlin. "Suggestion and Symbol." Nathaniel Hawthorne: An Introduction and Interpretation. Ed. John Mahoney. New York: Barnes and Noble, 1961. 121-133.

Psychomachia in Bliss County

Jack Pepper

English 1102/Literary Analysis, Researched

Conflicts between good and evil in fiction are often portrayed, not Just as a physical battle or shootout, but as a fight to win dominion over a character's soul. Stories depicting this spiritual confrontation use the classic description of evil coercing the central character by deception and temptation while the righteous forces promise redemption and salvation It appears that the concept of evil as an abiding, active force has almost vanished in sophisticated literature with modem narratives opting for current sociological and psychological explanations to obscure this ancient war for what is truly a struggle for the soul (Hoffman 81). This spiritual battle was once known as a *psychomachia.* Although Madison Jones's Last Things presents a surface structure which is naturalistic and fits all the demands of modem realism, there is, nonetheless, an allegorical *psychomachia* underlying the realistic plot.

The surface action of Jones's novel exhibits realism as nothing more and nothing less than the truthful treatment of material (Frye, Baker, Perkins 386). Realism demands viewing the world literally with nothing impossible, or hardly improbable, taking place. For example, Wendell Corbin appears to be a young man whose summer in Bliss County is highly distorted by drugs, alcohol abuse, and stress. All his perceived supernatural events could be the result of Wendell's stress, imagination, and guilt feelings about his deviant behavior. To the modem reader, the plot could appear to be blatantly realistic without any spiritual overtones.

However, the allegorical *psychomachia* that underlies the naturalistic plot becomes evident to the careful reader through many of the work's characters, its plot events, and its moral resolution. According to the critic C. S. Lewis, "Prudentius' poem, *Psychomachia,* written in Rome in the fifth century A.D., is the first piece of literature to use this term to describe this allegorical struggle between good and evil for the possession of a human soul" (66). In this type of allegory, there are characters who stand for the angelic forces as well as demonic ones. Similarly, while painting a very authentic picture of its characters, Last Things also depicts characters who act out a moral tale in a modem setting. Jason Farrow represents the definitive demonic force. In the full light of day he appears as a respectable businessman (like the Devil?) while in the darkness of night he is really the leader of a local drug cartel (Hoffman 81). Wendell sees through this facade and views Farrow as more than just a criminal kingpin as Lucifer himself Standing on Farrow's porch, awaiting his infernal orders, Wendell sees Farrow's face as that of the Satanic beast:

> toadlike on a neckless head up-rounded from rounded shoulders. No lips to the long straight mouth that looked as if a razor made it, and eyes without any lids. The bulging eyes were what he remembered best, with jewellike points of moonlight where pupils ought to be. *(L.T. 157)*

To the reader, then, Farrow can appear as Lucifer in starlight. However, Jones does not want to insist on his actually being the Devil, preferring to leave that interpretation to the reader (Jones, "Conv." 123). Farrow rules his evil, criminal empire through his minion Cat Bird, whom Jones himself once referred to as the "black servant of the Devil"(Jones, "Conv."123). Farrow uses Cat Bird as his watchful eye and his liaison with the corrupt townspeople, including the local sheriff. If Farrow has a loyal servant in Cat Bird, then Reverend Sears is Bliss County's "God-crazed preacher" who has been haunting Wendell since his adolescence (Hoffman 80). Sears appears to Wendell, even from a distance, like a tower whose eyes glare at him, not allowing him to move, and piercing his soul *(L. T.* 30). The Reverend's friend and benefactor, who shares his concern for Bliss County in decline, is Mrs. Emma Harker, an elderly woman who is presented as a pillar of the community and who symbolizes the old values and morals that the modem world seems to have cast aside (Cohen 97). Wendell senses her scrutiny, and her gaze makes him feel shameful *(L. T* 48). Wendell is "innocent" enough to be drawn into a sort of moral hell with Farrow tempting him with material riches while Sears's very physical presence threatens damnation (Childers 17). Reacting to his lust, greed, and Farrow's influence, Wendell loses control over his life. Having committed all the sins, including murder, Wendell feels his soul so overwhelmed that he must seek redemption through Sears. This *psychomachic* struggle forces Wendell to choose between God's grace, as dispensed by Sears, and spiritual death, the wages of Farrow and Co.

The novel's events chart out the *psychomachia* in a subtle but definitive manner. Wendell feels his return to Bliss County is a "fated thing; which obviously points toward the supernatural forces influencing his life *(L. T.* 1). Cat Bird, under orders from Farrow, sets Wendell up in a drug deal with the help of the local sheriff, leaving Wendell with the choice of working in Farrow's criminal organization or being sent to jail. This proves Farrow's power and control over the community and substantiates Mrs. Harker's statement, "I think it's the devil who is in charge now. Along with his minions" (*L. T.* 1). Wendell meets Tricia Harker, his neighbor, who in turn introduces him to her mother-in-law, Emma Harker. He soon realizes that Mrs. Harker is a thorn in Farrow's side and that she ultimately will have to be dealt with. As expected, Farrow orders Wendell to kill Mrs Harker. Wendell decides that he must use Tricia to kill her mother-in-law. By seducing Tricia, he gains her confidence and is allowed to "direct" her as he sees fit. During the planning and execution of the murder, Wendell handles Farrow's illegal business as he is instructed.

Wendell encounters Reverend Sears face-to-face at Mrs. Harker's viewing. For the first time he is actually introduced to him. As in his adolescence when he viewed him from a distance, Wendell senses Sears's spiritual presence from which he instinctively recoils. Wendell's guilt becomes apparent when he hallucinates that Sears actually visits his home and insists that he confess to Mrs Harker's murder. It is obvious even here that the demonic forces still grasp him, for he denies his sin to the phantom image of Sears.

Wendell is then sent to handle business for Farrow in the Cayman Islands where he plunges relentlessly into temptation and ultimate corruption. It is here that Wendell experiences a spiritual death and is reborn as a true nihilistic servant of darkness. His sadistic behavior with a local prostitute is reprehensible and surely proves the depth of evil's grip on him. Upon Wendell's return from the Cayman Islands, Tricia attempts suicide. Displaying what little good he can muster, Wendell tries to save her but fails. After her suicide, Wendell's conscience begins to eat away at him, causing him to question his unholy alliance with Jason Farrow.

Wendell's resurging conscience becomes the turning point of the novel as he is overwhelmed with fear for Sears's safety, who may be targeted as Farrow's next victim. Subsequently, Wendell seeks the aid of federal law enforcement agents, hoping to save Sears and bring down Farrow. Wendell is totally unequipped to deal with the level of Farrow's fury and his incredible tale, coupled with his lack of evidence, causes the officials to ignore his allegations. No one, including a local psychiatrist, can believe that a man of Jason Farrow's stature could possibly be involved in such heinous activities. Depressed by everyone's disbelief, Wendell seeks the solitude of his childhood home. Whether it is Wendell's self-induced paranoia or an evil presence in the house with him, the voice he hears barking, "You been belonging to me all your life," convinces him that the forces of darkness are waging a final attempt for his soul *(L. T* 182). This encounter is reinforced when Wendell returns to town and witnesses the burning of the Harker house, an arson he is sure is perpetrated by Farrow.

A *psychomachia* can depict the struggle of virtues and vices for the possession of the human soul in especially violent ways. This becomes apparent in this novel when Wendell takes matters into his own hands (Hermann 8). Feeling that he is delivering just and deserved punishment on Satan, Wendell attempts to burn

Farrow's house, a house which oozes with the very essence of Evil. Upon entering into what he believes is an empty house, Wendell realizes that he has indeed penetrated Satan's lair; he has crossed the threshold into Hell itself Wendell's vengeful frenzy is interrupted when he is struck on the back of the head and tossed out the upper window of this demonic nest.

Wendell awakens in the hospital crippled and with his eyesight temporarily impaired. According to Professor Carl Griffin, it appears that Jones is adamant that his characters, who are usually involved in moral struggles, pay for what they have done (Jones, "Conv." 29). But Wendell's blindness causes him to have a spiritual revelation, though not necessarily a religious conversion. By being blinded he begins to see more clearly on a spiritual level. Jones comments about the spiritually emerging Wendell that though "sort of left defeated," he, nevertheless, is "beginning to really see" (Jones, "Conv." 29). Wendell's spiritual insight includes the recognition that the events of the past summer have been the playing out of a *psychomachia,* in which his own soul has been the chief pawn:

> It was Wendell's experience of the following days that ultimately gave him his best reasons for rejecting the explanations of common sense. These reasons, together with others from both his recent and distant past, added up to a belief, practically a conviction, that he had been dealt with by forces of a superrational kind. Coincidences happened, all right. And a man's mind was capable of strange tricks and self-deceptions But taking things all together he found it difficult not to believe that his soul had been the object of some discarnate form of manipulation. *(L.T.* 187)

It becomes clear to Wendell, also, that Farrow's seduction of Bliss County will never allow his true identity to be revealed. Farrow convinces the townspeople that Wendell is nothing more than a delusional, drug-addicted crackpot, and plays down the threat to his power by not even pressing legal charges, convincing folks, once again, that he is a man of integrity and honor and not the "demon" Wendell claims he is. Sears comes to Wendell in the hospital seeking the truth and hoping to rescue Wendell from evil. Believing he barely escaped Satan's clutches with his life, and with his soul still intact, Wendell confesses his sins to his "spiritual father" and goes to live with Sears to assist in his religious crusades. Traveling the South with Sears, Wendell feels more hopeful, but his own faith remains incomplete.

Finally to heal his emotional and spiritual wounds, Wendell visits his father, whom he has not seen in five years. In a nursing home, his father appears oblivious to him but eventually makes the familiar gesture of smoking marijuana as they had done together on the Bliss County farm. Wendell is overwhelmed by his father's acknowledgment of his presence, and his eyes begin to tear, leaving Wendell, once again, momentarily unable to see and possibly on the verge of a new spiritual awakening.

Even though Jones's use of realism remains strong and vigorous in Last Things, the *psychomachia* emerges as a major influence in this classic tale of good and evil locked in deadly combat for the possession of a human soul. In this respect, the novel is unusual, as most modem writers tend to avoid accounts of spiritual struggles in favor of more overtly sensational materials. It is refreshing and impressive that one of today's first-rate authors possesses the boldness to express a spiritual tug-of-war at a time when the soul, God, and Satan are all considered passe'.

Works Cited

Childers, Joanne McEvilley. "Madison Jones-Place/Person The Effect of His Early Years on His Work." The Chattahoochee Review 17.1(1996): 13-17.

Cohen, Sandy. "Madison Jones." Dictionary of Literary Biography. Vol.152. Detroit: Gale, 1995. 92-98.

Frye, Northrop, Sheriden Baker, and George Perkins. The Harper Handbook to Literature. New York: Harper and Row, 1985.

Hermann, John P. Allegories of War. Ann Arbor: U of Michigan P, 1989.

Hoffman, William. "The Tempter Is Always With Us." The Chattahoochee Review 17.1(1996): 74-81.

Jones, Madison P. Last Things. Baton Rouge: Louisiana State UP, 1989.

Jones, Madison P., and Carl H. Griffin. "Somewhere Outside of Auburn Alabama: A Conversation with Madison Jones." The Chattahoochee Review 17.1 (1996): 116-137.

Lewis, C. S. The Allegory of Love. New York: Oxford UP, 1958.

"You will have written exceptionally well if, by skillful arrangement of your words, you have made an ordinary one seem original."

Horace

Miss Celie's Song

Amy Ross

English 1102/ Literary Analysis, Researched

Celie, in Alice Walker's *The Color Purple,* is a character who has to fight for everything she becomes. Celie lives in the rural South sometime during 1916 and 1942 (Towers 1814). In Celie's life she endures one painful moment followed by another, but in the end, these events do not define or ruin her. Quite the opposite happens. She is empowered to rise against her abusers and free herself from them. Celie reaches a point where she triumphs over all evil and breaks through as a free, successful and loving person despite enduring every possible soul-wrenching trauma that exists. Although Celie is uneducated, lacking in self-esteem, and isolated, she emerges as a strong individual who is extremely protective of her loved ones and uses her experiences to triumph over adversity.

Being uneducated limits Celie. A large contributing factor to her submission to men and the many years that she does not stand up for herself comes from her lack of education. Celie does not know much at all about sex or the birth of babies and doesn't find out until she has her first child. For instance, Celie says, "When I start to hurt and then my stomach start moving and then that little baby come out my pussy chewing on it fist you could have knock me over with a feather" (Walker 12). A large amount of confusion exists in Celie's life because she does not have basic knowledge that most people have. Celie's absence of knowledge about her own pregnancy is quite believable considering the circumstances in which she was raised. Many black women of that time were told lies about where babies came from (Harris 1820). Celie gets the small amount of information that she does have about her own body almost as if by accident. Celie writes, "A girl at church say you git big if you bleed every month. I don't bleed no more" (Walker 15). Celie does not comprehend that she is permanently sterile and will never again be able to have children. And she certainly does not understand why or how it happened. Celie does not even understand her own hysterectomy. A girl at church has to explain to her that she will never be able to have children. Ross writes, "Even this knowledge, personal as it is, comes to Celie second hand" (71). Celie is lacking in formal education as well as education in life. This is evidenced in the letters she writes. Celie spells everything phonetically and makes an enormous number of grammatical and punctuation errors. She is able to express herself through her writing, but the writing demonstrates how uneducated she is.

Celie's lack of education causes much pain in her life. When her sister Nettie is taken from her, she loses all hope for becoming educated. And it is this lack of education that continues to cause her pain when she finally gets to see the letters Nettie had been sending all the years. Celie feels a little better once she learns that Nettie is alive and has not forgotten her, but she would be even more comforted if she could picture where Nettie is (physically) as evidenced when she states, "I don't know where England at. Don't know where Africa at either. So I still don't know where Nettie at" (Walker 114). While Celie is relieved finally to receive the news that her long lost sister is alive and well, her lack of education hinders her from feeling as happy as she might. Selzer quotes Celie when she says, "What matters about not knowing 'where Africa at' -- according to Celie -- is not knowing 'where Nettie at'" (1).

Secondary to the abuse and habitual violence Celie endures is her desperate lack of self-esteem. She is brutalized by the man she thinks is her father and feels as if it is her fault that she is raped. At the very beginning of the novel, after being warned by her stepfather about telling anyone but God about being raped, Celie writes, "I am I have always been a good girl" (Walker 11). Celie thinks that since her stepfather has brutally raped her, she is no longer a "good girl." Celie crossed out "I am" and writes, "I always have been a good girl," because she feels she has done something to deserve being raped (Proudfit 17). Celie's father does not stop at taking away all of Celie's dignity by raping her. When Albert is inquiring about marrying Nettie, her father quickly tells him that he can't have her, but he could certainly take Celie. In Celie's letter describing the day

Mr. ___ comes over to see her Pa, she overhears them talking:

> . . . I can't let you have Nettie . . . . But I can let you have Celie . . . . She ain't fresh tho, but I spect you know that. She spoiled. Twice. But you don't need no fresh woman no how . . . . Mr. _____ Don't say nothing. I stop crying I'm so surprise. She ugly. He say. But she ain't no stranger to hard work. And she clean. And God done fixed her. You can do everything just like you want and she ain't gonna make you feed or clothe it. (Walker 17-18).

The way Celie's stepfather talks about her is dehumanizing. These men talk about her and make it sound as if they are selling a farm animal or a slave. They think of her and treat her as less than human. To them, she is no better than a slave or a farm animal. She is the means through which work gets done and no more. And these two men, her father and her future husband, are the ones that should love her and care for her more than anyone in the world. Pa and Mr.____ are the main reasons she feels no self-worth. Ever since she can remember, she has been treated in this manner. Celie's lack of self-esteem is a major part of why it takes her so long to stand up for herself and stop her abuse. She develops a feeling of worthiness before she can overcome the abuse. Hankinson agrees, stating that "Pa's relinquishment of Celie to Mr.___ differs very little from the way one might relinquish cattle" (1). Celie's stepfather "presents her as less than a whole woman to her future husband," and one can assume that her Pa's attitude does not help any chance that her husband will ever treat her as any more than subhuman (Ross 75). Adams explains that Celie's Pa sells her "into a virtual state of slavery" to a man that is almost a complete stranger (3412). It is amazing that Celie discovers any sense of self-worth after enduring this type of degrading treatment from the two men in her life who are supposed to care the most and protect her.

Celie's lack of self-esteem is evident later when she is talking to Harpo and explaining to him about the difference between herself and Sofia. Celie is very telling in her thoughts when she says, "Some womens can't be beat, I say. Sofia one of them" (Walker 66). It is apparent that Celie believes that although not all women can be beat (like Sofia), she is one that can be beaten; therefore, she is. The reason Sofia can not be beaten is that she will not allow it. Sofia respects herself too much to allow any man to lay a hand on her, much to Harpo's dismay.

Shug inadvertently helps Celie with her low self-esteem when she writes a song for her and sings it in public. Celie writes about Shug's performance: "She say this song I'm bout to sing is call Miss Celie's song. Cause she scratch it out of my head when I was sick. First she hum it a little, like she do at home. Then she sing the words . . . . First time somebody made something and name it after me" (Walker 75). Celie has never experienced anyone appreciating her or caring about her. She expresses this when she remarks how nobody had ever named anything after her. Shug is the first person in Celie's life who tries to communicate to Celie how special she is and that her existence matters. Ross explains, "Celie lacks an identity. Shug awakens Celie's desire for identity most explicitly when she sings a song she has written for Celie . . . . The act of naming something after Celie assures the integrity of Celie herself; she must be something to be the subject of a song" (76-77).

Celie's lack of self-esteem is further shown by her comment to Shug, "Nobody ever love me" (Walker 109). Celie, in her heart, believes that no one loves her. She has experienced so much violence and abuse in her life and has made the assumption that anyone so abused and violated so often must deserve it and, therefore, must be a bad person. But Shug steps forward and tells Celie, "I love you, Miss Celie" (Walker 109). Shug becomes someone for Celie to tell her past hurts to, and Shug shows Celie how to be loved. Shug tries to make it clear to Celie that no matter how people treat her, she is worthy of being loved. Shug helps Celie develop by becoming a surrogate mother, in a sense, for her. Shug provides Celie with "unconditional love," "female bonding," and a safe environment (Proudfit 23). Shug nurtures Celie and helps her become a stable, complete grown up.

Celie's lack of self-esteem is evidenced by her writing the letters. Celie is so embarrassed about her Pa raping her that she feels she cannot tell anyone. Her sister Nettie later writes to Celie about it: "I remember one time you said your life made you feel so ashamed you couldn't even talk about it to God, you had to write it down, bad as you thought your writing was" (Walker 122). Celie doesn't understand yet that there is nothing to be ashamed about and that even though her father raped her, it is not a reflection of her self-worth. Her sister even remarks about Celie's feeling that not only could she not tell anyone, but she also felt that she couldn't even write her sorrows down very well. Celie is too scared and embarrassed to tell anyone about her father raping her, so she writes to God (Proudfit 17).

Besides having no feelings of self-worth, Celie is isolated from the world with the exception of her family. This isolation adds to Celie's problems because she has nothing to compare her experiences to, no way to see with her own eyes that things are not all bad everywhere. Very early on in her letters Celie writes, "Don't nobody come see us" (Walker 12). Celie is lonely, in a sense divided from her sisters since she is forced into the position of caretaker for all of her younger brothers and sisters, and she is completely separated from any other ideas or opportunities to have caring people in her life. Celie is "isolated and alone, despite the numbers of family members and others impinging upon her world" (Davis 1818). Because Celie is isolated, she is kept from understanding the depth of her submission to the male authority and from escaping the men that once held her down. Because Celie is so detached from the world throughout most of her life, she learns how to be strong by herself, and her painful isolation ends up adding to her character.

Celie is not only physically isolated from the outside world, but after years and years of abuse and violence, she begins to feel isolated from the only person she could pour her heart out to: God. After reading a letter from Nettie and finding out that the man she always thought was her father really isn't, that her real father was lynched, that her children are not actually products of incest, and that Shug is going to take her away to Tennessee, Celie exclaims to God, "You must be sleep" (Walker 163). Celie does not understand how a God that is paying any attention at all could let her be continually abused and degraded and let her life end up the way it has so far. Now Celie feels isolated from the God she has always viewed in a traditional sense. But when Shug gives Celie a new way to think about God, it is as if she has freed Celie from this uncaring, oblivious, "deef" God that she has been writing to for so long. Hankinson notes that "this iron fisted God keeps Celie in constant fear of being punished, bridling her subordination; because Celie has been discarded by this 'old white man'. . . , she is left at the bottom of the world's pecking order, as she is black, poor, female, and unattractive" (2). Celie again tells of her frustration with her traditional view of God:

> Anyhow, I say, the God I been praying and writing to is a man. And act just like all the other mens I know. Trifling, forgitful and lowdown.
>
> She [Shug] say, Miss Celie, You better hush. God might hear you.
>
> Let 'im hear me, I say. If he ever listened to poor colored women the world would be a different place, I can tell you. (Walker 175)

Celie feels as if God has abandoned her just like all the other men in her life have. How could a God that pays any attention to her just stand by and watch her go through the abuse, rape, incest and emotional deprivation that she has endured all of her life? Until Shug gives her a new way to view God, Celie feels isolated from Him. Hankinson writes, "When Shug teaches Celie that God is in everything, including the flowers, wind and water . . . and God is in her, and she is inherently connected to everything . . . , her sense of fear and of being judged dissolves," and she is no longer isolated from God and the world (3).

Due to the isolation and abuse Celie endures, Celie must be strong to be able to survive. She overcomes extensive pain, abuse, and violence with strength and dignity. Celie learns how to remove herself from her own body at times to endure the things she must. She writes,

> He beat me like he beat the children. Cept he don't never hardly beat them. He say, Celie, git the belt. The children be outside the room peeking through the cracks. It

> all I can do not to cry. I make myself wood. I say to myself, Celie, you a tree. That's how come I know trees fear man. (Walker 30)

Celie's husband treats her as a slave, but she endures it and becomes even stronger. She is humiliated and degraded in the worst ways possible and is treated as if she is worthless, but due to her amazing inner strength, she comes through with grace and with dignity. Because of all the emotional trauma Celie has been through in her life, she is able to remove herself from her feelings (Proudfit 20). It is her way of coping. Ross writes of Celie: "Strength can come from enduring oppression with as much dignity as possible and then rising to denounce it" (80). This is a recurring theme in many of the letters. Celie becomes so strong from having endured the abuse that she finally gains the strength to rise up against it and save herself.

Throughout Celie's life she protects the people that she loves, mainly Shug and Nettie. From the time Celie is very young, she protects Nettie from sexual abuse by their father. Celie writes, "I ast him to take me instead of Nettie while our new mammy sick. But he just ast me what I'm talking bout. I tell him I can fix myself up for him. I duck into my room and come out wearing horsehair, feathers, and a pair of our new mammy high heel shoes. He beat me for dressing trampy but he do it to me anyway" (Walker 17). Celie diverts Alphonso's attention away from Nettie in order to save her from his sexual abuse. This characteristic is part of what ties Nettie so much to Celie. She knows what her sister did for her, and she understands how hard it must have been for Celie to protect her.

Celie is protective of Nettie in other ways, too. She is forced from a very young age to assume the responsibility of raising Nettie. She tells of comforting Nettie in a letter to God: "I'll take care of you. With God help" (Walker 13). Because Celie's mother goes crazy and Alphonso does not have the temperament for nurturing young children, we can assume that Celie takes on the role of mothering Nettie and her other siblings at a very young age (Proudfit 19). Celie advises Nettie to study very hard to become an educated person because Celie does not want to see Nettie end up in a similar situation (Proudfit 32). When Nettie comes to live with Celie and

Mr.____, Celie takes care of Nettie until Mr.____ forces Nettie to leave. Celie is the one who guides Nettie to the Reverend Mr.____ and his wife, an action that saves Nettie from a fate similar to Celie's. Corrine and Samuel educate Nettie and teach her how to live a completely different type of life, free from abuse and violence.

Most importantly, Celie is triumphant over the abusers in her life. From her strength and ability to endure all that she goes through, Celie finally draws "the courage to speak" from deep down in her soul, and she frees herself from the cruel and heartless treatment of Mr.____ (Ross 69). After Celie finds that Mr.____ has been hiding Nettie's letters for all of those years, and Shug announces at the dinner table that Celie is coming with her to Memphis, Mr.____ cannot believe his ears. He says that "Over [his] dead body" will Celie leave (181). Celie finally stands up for herself in her first words spoken against her husband: "You a lowdown dog. . . . It's time to leave you and enter into the Creation. And your dead body just the welcome mat I need" (181). Celie liberates herself for the first time. She makes it clear that she is not going to stand for his despicable treatment of her anymore. In just a few sentences, Celie is free.

She continues on to say, "Every lick you hit me you will suffer twice, I say. Then I say, you better stop talking because all I'm telling you ain't coming just from me. Look like when I open my mouth air rush in and shape words" (187). Celie is vigorously expressing her freedom now. She lets the years of frustration and pain pour from her heart. She proceeds to tell him, "I curse you, I say. What you mean? He say. I say until you do right by me, everything you touch will crumble" (187). Celie has done it. She has used the power of words to stand up for herself for the first time in her life. She also lets Mr.______know that she expects to be "done right by." She has made the giant leap from victim to survivor. Later Celie "further recognizes the power of speech when her curse on Albert sinks him into a life-threatening depression" (Ross 80). Celie's curse on Albert is removed and his "regeneration begun only when he does what Celie demanded--return Nettie's letters to her" (Ross 80).

In the novel *The Color Purple,* we watch Celie go through her life, full of abuse and violence. These experiences shape her, and her strength is tested every single day. But rather than give up and lose all hope of ever overcoming her miserable situation, Celie becomes stronger and stronger until the day arrives when she can denounce her oppressors and overcome them. The theme "love redeems and meanness kills" is played out throughout Celie's life (Adams 3408; Prescott 450). In the end it is Celie who triumphs and is liberated. Although Celie has to work extra hard because she is so uneducated and isolated from the world, through her strength and bonds with the people that care for her, Celie "finds the courage to speak" and sets herself free (Ross 69).

Works Cited

Adams, Timothy Dow. "Alice Walker." Critical Survey of Long Fiction. Ed. Frank N. Magill. Vol. 7. Pasadena: Salem, 1991. 3407-3415. 8 vols.

Davis, Thadious M. "Alice Walker's Celebration of Self in Southern Generations." Women Writers of the Contemporary South. Ed. Peggy Whitman Penshaw. Oxford: UP of Mississippi, 1984. 39-53. Excerpted and rpt. in Black Literature Criticism. Ed. James P. Draper. Vol. 3. Detroit: Gale, 1992. 1813-1827. 3 vols.

Hankinson, Stacie Lynn. "From Monotheism to Pantheism: Liberation from Patriarchy in Alice Walker's The Color Purple." Midwest Quarterly 38 (Spring 1997): 320-28. Periodical Abstracts. Online. 12 Oct. 1997.

Harris, Trudier. "On The Color Purple: Stereotypes and Silence." Black American Literature Forum 18.4 (Winter 1984): 155-61. Excerpted and rpt. in Black Literature Criticism. Ed. James P. Draper. Vol. 3. Detroit: Gale, 1992. 1819-22. 3 vols.

Prescott, Peter S. "A Long Road to Liberation." Newsweek 21 June 1982: 67-8. Rpt. in Contemporary Literary Criticism. Ed. Jean C. Stine. Vol. 27. Detroit: Gale, 1984. 449-50.

Proudfit, Charles L. "Celie's Search for Identity: A Psychoanalytic Developmental Reading of Alice Walker's The Color Purple." Contemporary Literature 32 (Spring 1991): 12-35.

Ross, Daniel W. "Celie in the Looking Glass: The Desire for Selfhood in The Color Purple." Modern Fiction Studies 34 (Spring 1988): 69-83.

Selzer, Linda. "Race and Domesticity in The Color Purple." African American Review 29 (Spring 1995): 67-82. Periodical Abstracts. Online. 12 Oct. 1997.

Towers, Robert. "Good Men Are Hard to Find." The New York Review of Books 12 Aug. 1982: 35-6. Excerpted and rpt. in Black Literature Criticism. Ed. James P. Draper. Vol. 3. Detroit: Gale, 1992. 1814. 3 vols.

Walker, Alice. The Color Purple. New York: Washington Square, 1982.

◆◆◆

"Advice is seldom welcome,
and those who want it the most
always like it the least."

Earl of Chesterfield

Rousseau's Elevation of The Social Contract

David B. Kirkus

English 2305/Literary Analysis, Researched

The concept of a social contract seems to be a common thread through the works of many of the great eighteenth century philosophes. Many of these pacts revolve around the central idea that human life originated in a theoretical state of nature. This condition exists where, "stripped of artificial or acquired characteristics, man [sic] appears as an animal, existing at a level of pure sensation, and able to satisfy the simple needs of food and rest in the immediate environment" (Broome 36). Thomas Hobbes speculates that humanity eventually progresses from this state to pledge all power to an absolute monarch. Thus, authority comes from the people rather than from God, as is the case in a Divine Right monarchy, yet those being ruled still enjoy no voice in the regulations affecting their own lives. John Locke's philosophy takes the contract a step further, stating that, developing out of a state of nature, humankind creates a contract forming a society that does not surrender all rights. This agreement, unlike that of Hobbes, places an obligation on the ruler to protect the people's rights; the populace can overthrow the leader if it is their will to do so. This evolution of democratic thought continues to evolve and culminates with the opinions of Jean-Jacques Rousseau. His political masterpiece The Social Contract provides a pure example of one Enlightenment era philosopher taking the themes of his period to a new plateau. It represents the most democratic of all social contracts. Every member of society surrenders all rights to everyone else, creating rule by the general will.

Emerging in a time of powerful Divine Right monarchs and conquering leaders, any assertion of democratic thought, indeed, draws much disdain from the ruling class in question. Though The Social Contract shares Rousseau's opinions on the way government ought to be rather than focusing on the inadequacies of established administrations, it became a catalyst, speeding up the frequency of events that inevitably result in democracy. Shortly after its release, the book found itself banned throughout Europe, being burned publicly in many large cities (Mason 28). However, Rousseau's message spread quickly, and many great leaders of the French Revolution eventually championed his ideals. Consequently, these principles must be profound for an event of such historical importance to hinge upon their declaration.

Throughout his statement of these principles, Rousseau seems generally irritated with the individual's role in society and proposes a method for advancing the common good of all people as a whole while still maintaining the freedom of each member of the society. He declares: "Each of us puts his person and all his power in common under the supreme direction of the general will, and, in our corporate capacity, we receive each member as an indivisible part of the whole" (15). This statement brings new recognition to the rights of those who, previously regarded only as subjects to some remote ruler, now begin to consider themselves citizens with privileges of their own. Under this type of agreement, "the people alone have the sovereign and inalienable right to legislate," not those who find themselves in comfortable government positions due to their lineage (Saccamano 737).

For this principle to work properly, "every valid political society must be based on the free participation of its members" (Grimsley 91). Many political writings of the Enlightenment era exhibit this essential belief, but none to the extent of that in The Social Contract. Rousseau requires a total shift in the power base: the aristocrats must concede much of their authority so that they will be equal, in a political sense, to the commoners. This surrender must be complete so that the power lies within everyone, as a whole, and the individual has no direct influence against the general will.

Also, Rousseau appears to attribute infallibility to the majority since he believes that no one should be allowed to question its determination. However, he does imply that "what makes the will general is not so much the number of voices as the common interest uniting them" (Gough 173). He gives more significance to the quality of the decisions that society makes than to the number of people adopting a particular idea. This certainly does not suggest that everyone will approve of the will and, in fact, indicates that individuals will deviate from the prevailing notion at times. To compensate for any divergence, Rousseau notes:

> In order then that the social compact may not be an empty formula, it tacitly includes the undertaking, which alone can give force to the rest, that whoever refuses to obey the general will shall be compelled to do so by the whole body. This means nothing less than that he [sic] will be forced to be free. (18)

In essence, he is saying that "the general will never damages individual interests because it never decides anything but the non-contentious" (Gough 170). Therefore, since the general will always acts in the best interest of individual freedom, individuals, acting alone, cannot propose anything for their own benefit that would not also benefit the whole community.

With the principle of the general will as a guiding light, Rousseau also offers many other ideas that now seem fundamental to the workings of a démocratic government. The exchange of the social contract states the "advantages of civil society over the state of nature and stresses increased liberty and equality" (Simon-Ingram 137). He names many of these liberties explicitly at various stages of his work. Rousseau introduces a system of voting that would allow comparison of opinions according to the general will (105). He discusses censorship and concludes that, since no two individuals share the exact opinions of right and wrong, it has no place in a legitimate society. He also proclaims that the institution of religion by the state leads only to it enslaving those who will not conform. These and other democratic thoughts appear constantly throughout The Social Contract.

Rousseau obviously displays a certain amount of courage by publishing his opinions in such a time. His political theory lends new merit to the cause of democracy, especially in France and later in the United States. Though his idea of government by the general will is much more philosophical than practical, it certainly sheds new light on the rights of citizens to speak for themselves. Rousseau himself admits that his views cannot hold true in every country, but he argues that they are a fundamentally sound basis for reform. The idea of a social contract is certainly not unique to the writings of Rousseau, as many other treatises date prior to his. Yet he expands upon these other works, criticizing some, celebrating others, while building upon all. The result of his lifelong dedication to the subject is a monumental text that brings new meaning to the rights of citizens and challenges governments with the ideas of liberty, freedom, and justice.

Works Cited

Broome, J. H. Rousseau: A Study of His Thought. London: Edward Arnold, 1963.

Gough, J. W. The Social Contract. Oxford: Clarendon, 1963.

Grimsley, Ronald. The Philosophy of Rousseau. Oxford: Oxford UP, 1973.

Mason, John Hope. The Indispensable Rousseau. London: Quartet, 1979.

Rousseau, Jean-Jacques. The Social Contract. The Social Contract and Discourses. Ed. G. D. H. Cole. New York: Dutton, 1950. 1-141.

Saccamano, Neil. "Rhetoric, Consensus, and the Law in Rousseau's *Contrat Social*." MLN 107 (Sept. 1992): 730-51.

Simon-Ingram, Julia. "Expanding the Social Contract: Rousseau, Gender, and the Problem of Judgment." Comparative Literature 43 (Spring 1991): 134-49.

♦ ♦ ♦

"Of all the arts in which the wise excel,
Nature's chief masterpiece is writing well."

John Sheffield, Duke of Buckingham

The Meticulously Manufactured Reality of *Titanic*

Sara C. deVarennes

Film 1301/Film Review

James Cameron's *Titanic,* well on its way to a gross of one billion dollars, continues to draw hundreds of thousands of viewers each week. Though the movie is in its tenth week of release, people still remain captivated by the love story of Jack Dawson and Rose DeWitt Bukater. Yet, this film does not tell the average Hollywood love story. This story, though fictional, centers around an actual event which has intrigued people all over the world for over 85 years. The historical validity, the magic of the characters, and the audience's own desire for such a romance brings *Titanic* to life. However, the reality is not accidental. Every word, every person, and every detail of the movie have a specific purpose. Cameron includes only the necessary elements, yet he leaves nothing out. He literally manufactures people, places, and events to seem like real life. The carefully planned *mise-en-scene,* special effects, and music contribute greatly to the sense of reality in Cameron's *Titanic.*

Cameron first draws his audience into the historical reality of *Titanic* during the calculated visit to the actual ship at the bottom of the ocean. The camera goes directly into the heart of the ship. The audience members see ornate furniture, candleholders, chandeliers and much more. Though these things appear much different than they did in 1912, people can still appreciate the elegance and beauty of such a ship. The audience probably tries to imagine what the ship looked like so many years ago. For this reason, people connect with Rose Calvert, a *Titanic* survivor. Images of the sunken ship cause her to flash back to her own memory of the appearance of the ship in 1912. The audience begins to associate real people and real emotions with the mysterious wreck at the bottom of the ocean.

Next, Cameron brings his audience further into the story of *Titanic* by introducing the two main characters, Jack Dawson and Rose DeWitt Bukater. Jack Dawson first appears in a small pub playing cards with his friends. He wears simple clothes and uses simple language. Immediately, the audience relates to Jack as the everyman of *Titanic*. Rose DeWitt Bukater, on the other hand, represents what the everyman desires. She lives the life of wealth and glamour. The audience first sees Rose as she steps out of a high-class carriage wearing high-class clothing. The camera pans from her feet to her face, partially hidden by a large hat. The large hat that Rose wears and the way she holds her body create a sense of mystery and intrigue. The everyman desires that which he cannot fully grasp or understand.

Cameron then uses an intrusive camera to bring the audience into the developing relationship between Jack and Rose. During their first encounter, the camera usually holds their heads and bodies close together creating a sense of sexual tension from the beginning. For most of the movie, Jack and Rose appear together in shots. The camera almost always allows the audience to be a part of the relationship between the two lovers. The head shots and three-quarter shots keep the characters close to the audience. Cameron includes some full shots, especially during the dance scene in the third-class level of the ship. However, these full body shots do not separate the characters from each other or from the audience. Jack and Rose move during dance as one unit. Likewise, during the love scene, Jack and Rose are in the shot together. The camera never focuses on either individual. The camera stays very close, including the audience in this long awaited scene.

Aside from realistic characters, today's latest technology allows Cameron to create an authentic depiction of the events of April 1912. The magic of *Titanic* involves modern cinematic technology. Models, computer animation, and lots of imagination give the movie a prestigious place in cinematic history. Cameron did not build a complete full-scale replica of the ship, and he did not really sail his replica on the Atlantic Ocean. Instead, models and computer animation create many of *Titanic*'s memorable scenes. As the ship leaves Southampton, the audience sees a full shot of the length of the ship with people on deck. The ship is actually a model, and the people are animated by computer. Later, Jack and his friend look over the stern of the ship at a family of swimming dolphins. In this scene, the dolphins are real, but computer animation provides the front of the ship and the moving water. The famous kiss scene took months to plan and develop. The beautiful sunset, the sparkling ocean, and the movement of the boat are all products of computer animation. In reality, the ship sinks on a very cold evening in the middle of the Atlantic Ocean. However, the set of *Titanic* exists somewhere in Mexico. Computer animation later added the visibly frosty breath of characters on the cold night in 1912. Though today's audiences are quite sophisticated, computer animation blends well with the tangible elements of a film to make the special effects difficult to identify. The special effects in *Titanic* appear as reality.

The specially composed music of *Titanic* further charms and draws the audience into the unfolding story. The music is timeless, suggesting that people in 1912 were not much different from people today. The musical composer, James Horner, uses both a traditional full orchestra and a more modern synthesizer in the musical score to cross over any generational and/or cultural differences. The universality of the music of *Titanic* adds much to the emotional effect. The tone of the music expresses the feelings of the characters and allows the audience an even more personal view into the lives of Jack and Rose. The music also gives the film a sense of unity. The same melody recurs throughout the film. Though none of the music in the actual film includes words, many audience members may be familiar with the popular love song performed by Celine Dion that is played on the radio. The recurring instrumental melody reminds the audience of the love song and the developing love story.

Cameron's audience becomes an actual part of the unfolding story of *Titanic*. The audience seems to be another group aboard the ship, sharing in the experience of characters like Jack and Rose. As the ship begins to sink, Cameron's audience is too involved in the story to jump overboard. Instead, they vicariously experience the events and the emotions on screen. Unlike 1,500 people on April 14, 1912, Cameron's audience sits safely on a lifeboat as *Titanic* sinks before their eyes. *Titanic*'s survivors held the memory of the disaster for their entire lives. Cameron's audience will hold the memory of the film as well. The disaster, the glamour, the characters, and, of course, the love will linger along time in the movie viewers' memories.

◆◆◆

"Writers, like teeth, are divided into incisors and grinders."

Walter Bagehot

Zen Buddhism: Footsteps to Enlightenment

Jon Hegidio

Religion 1301

As the Zen Buddhist student enters the *zendo* (meditation room), he ponders the assigned question given to him, "What did your original face look like before your parents were born?" (Hopfe 152). A whole lifetime in the pursuit of becoming a Zen Buddhist has boiled down to this question. The frustrated student has spent his every waking thought trying to make sense out of a senseless riddle. During breakfast, meditation, daily chores, and sleep, this question has weighed on his conscience. "How will this ridiculous riddle help me fulfill my destiny towards enlightenment?" he wonders. The master sits there in the center of the room and acknowledges the student as he bows before entering. The scholar bows again before seating himself and then peers into the master's eyes with total confidence and respect. "The third time is a charm," he thinks as he begins to impress the master with his answer. The disciple's eyes light up with pride and assurance as the final words depart his mouth and make their way to the master. He is totally confident that he has solved the riddle. The master lowers his eyebrows, sighs, and confirms the student's failure with one simple nod of his head. The youth is dismissed from the *zendo* with the *Koan* still unresolved and his path to enlightenment obscured by the mists of his present confusion. He does realize, however, that behind his quest and present dilemma lies a tradition which emerged some five-hundred years before the birth of Christ.

Buddhism began around the sixth century BC in India with the birth of Prince Gautama who later became the founder of Buddhism The prince was then known by his followers and to the Indian people as Buddha. The Buddha taught that ignorance--created by our greed, hate, and delusion-- prevents us from realizing that we are all naturally enlightened ("Zen"). At the time, Buddhism practiced solitude and contemplation as a means to achieve *Nirvana* (the ultimate goal of Buddhist practice). *Nirvana* is the loss of one's self in ultimate bliss and is usually induced through deep and prolonged meditation. The spread of Buddhism then began its travels to China where modifications of this practice continued.

The immigration of Buddhism from India to China came through the twenty-eighth Patriarch of Indian Buddhism named Bodhidharma, who, in turn, became the first Patriarch of Chinese Buddhism and created a new form of Buddhism called Ch'an ("Zen"). Bodhidharma's Ch'an Buddhism proclaimed that meditation was the path to achieve enlightenment and that there was no preliminary training or elaborate preparation necessary to realize the "Way" (Hopfe 151). While Ch'an Buddhism had its effect on the Chinese culture, it did not flourish until it reached Japan in the twelfth century. Once situated in Japan, Ch'an Buddhism took off to new levels and began a promising future within the Japanese culture where it was to be known as Zen Buddhism. Here, the intrusive and spontaneous route to enlightenment was reemphasized, and reason and intellect disparaged as obstructions to the *Nirvana* experience.

The main practice of Zen revolves around *zazen* (meditation), in an effort to reach *satori* (the sudden event of enlightenment or *Nirvana).* Perhaps the most unusual aspect of Zen Buddhism is how to attempt or achieve enlightenment. Several techniques are used to accomplish this ultimate goal such as meditation, paradoxical riddles, and/or startling noises. Often a Zen student is given a *Koan* (case study), by the master in order to maintain focus during meditation. These riddles usually make no sense but, nevertheless, aid students by distracting them from concentrating and relying too much on reason: "You have heard the sound of the clapping of two hands, but what is the sound of one hand clapping?" (Hopfe 152*)* This *Koan* and many other *Koans* alike have guided students to the road of ecstasy. Once a student thinks he has solved the *Koan,* he arranges for a private interview *(roshi)* with one of the Zen masters. The student is required to bow upon entrance into the room and once again before sitting in front of the master. The master will nod, give a hand gesture, or ring a bell to let the student know that he has not provided the correct answer (Miura and Sasaki 29). The Zen teacher is said to posses the ability to discern whether a student has or has not been enlightened by the student's aura or the way he now carries himself. The master *must certify* the *satori* experience! (Principles and Practices of Zen).

Once a month Zen students undergo an intense meditation program called a *sesshin* which usually lasts anywhere from seven to ten days. During *sesshins,* students are not allowed to talk, read, or interact with other students. Their meditation sessions increase from nine to ten hours daily and sometimes continue through the night. Some monasteries provide chin rests that are attached to the students' robes to help them get a little sleep through the night (Blackstone 90). During daytime meditation, the students are monitored by one of the teachers in the monastery. Some teachers carry a long flat wooden board called a k*yosaku* and strike the students when they are not meditating properly or nodding off into sleep. This technique of discipline is said to have startled students into enlightenment from shock while other students' request this "punishment" in order to stay refreshed or to help the circulation of their blood (Principles and Practices of Zen). Outside of meditation, the students and monks help around the monastery by providing manual labor such as keeping the grounds or washing dishes.

Once a student or monk has achieved enlightenment, what is there left to accomplish? Several monks stay behind to help their fellow students achieve enlightenment and are referred to as *Bodhisattvas. Bodhisattvas* postpone their achievement *of Nirvana* following their death and share their merit with humankind by helping others along the road to *Nirvana* (Suzuki 414). Other followers leave the monastery and continue the lives they once led. Regardless if they chose to stay or leave, their enlightenment task has been fulfilled, and they experience the world through different eyes. The sharp line between *Samsara* (the cycle of existence) and *Nirvana* is now erased and the two realms are seen as manifesting one another. Buddha's single vision will have been achieved by his disciple twenty-five hundred years after his death, and the oneness of all experience will again have been reconfirmed.

The road to enlightenment for the Zen Buddhist is not an easy task to accomplish and requires the utmost patience, concentration, and discipline. Some monks devote their entire lives to this Buddhist practice and are still are unable to achieve *satori,* yet their faith and perseverance continue to push them closer to the point of oneness and the "Void." It does not matter then if one remains in the monastery or goes off alone as long as one is free of attachment to all earthly things and to all images, even the image of Lord Buddha himself (Blackstone 92).

Our young disciple shrugs as he begins his morning chores in the kitchen. He is tired, confused, and ready to give up. As he approaches his manual duties in an absentminded fashion, a distant sound of several chirping crickets echoes throughout the room which provides a harmonious rhythm to the sweeping task at hand. Suddenly, he begins to feel a soothing and peaceful wave travel through his body. His brain feels as if it is "turning over" inside his head. At last, he views the room and his own body from above. And then there is no body and no room--only the blissful Void of Oneness. Our student, engulfed in light and splendor, realizing what may have just occurred, begins to sprint out of the kitchen and through the courtyard determined to rendezvous with the one person who has the power to confirm -- the Zen Master.

Works Cited

Blackstone, J. Zen for Beginners. New York: Writers and Readers, 1992.

Hopfe, Lewis M. Religions of the World. 6th ed. New York: Macmillan, 1994.

Miura, Isshu and Ruth F. Sasaki. The Zen Koan. New York: Harcourt Brace, 1993.

Principles and Practices of Zen. NHK. Japanese Broadcasting Corp. Videocassette. Films for the Humanities and Sciences, 1988.

Suzuki, Daisetz. Zen and Japanese Culture. Princeton: Princeton UP, 1993.

"Zen." Chapel Hill, N.C. : Chapel Hill Zen Group. Available: http://www.intrx.netlchzg/#Zen

◆◆◆

"Talent alone cannot make a good writer.
There must be a man behind the book."

Ralph Waldo Emerson

List of Contributors

Ashley Abercrombie
Sequoyah High School
Canton, Georgia

David Ajoy
Jonesboro High School
Jonesboro, Georgia

Michael Bannister
Chattahoochee High School
Alpharetta, Georgia

Nancy Baumgarten
Chattahoochee High School
Alpharetta, Georgia

Robert Benjamin
Milton High School
Alpharetta, Georgia

Adis Bojcic
Southwest High School
Fort Worth, Texas

Katherine Bollan
St. Johnsbury Academy
St. Johnsbury, Vermont

Scott Campbell
Milton High School
Alpharetta, Georgia

Carrie Collins
Snellville, Georgia

Billy Cowart
Berkmar High School
Lilburn, Georgia

Sara C. deVarennes
South Gwinnett High School
Snellville, Georgia

Paige Eberhart
Roswell, Georgia

Ryan Fields
Stephens County High School
Toccoa, Georgia

Alfonzo C. Ford II
H. B. Plant High School
Tampa, Florida

Iman Foufa
Lycee Regional Montgrand
Marseille, France

Habtemariam G. Gidey
Eritrea

Andrew Gilley
Norcross, Georgia

Deborah Goldman
Jonesboro Senior High School
Jonesboro, Georgia

Neil Graf
Ben Franklin Academy
Atlanta, Georgia

Jennifer Graybeal
Meadowcreek High School
Norcross, Georgia

Danielle Grillaert
South Forsyth High School
Cumming, Georgia

Jon Hegidio
Henderson High School
Chamblee, Georgia

Pamela Hopkins
Shiloh High School
Stone Mountain, Georgia

Jill Huang
Roswell High School
Roswell, Georgia

Jennifer Jones
Norcross High School
Norcross, Georgia

Lois Jones
East Robertson High School
Orlinda, Tennessee

Laura Judy
Roswell High School
Roswell, Georgia

David B. Kirkus
Covington, Georgia

Cecilia LaBar
Chattahoochee High School
Alpharetta, Georgia

Katie Lowder
Fremont High School
Sunnyvale, California

Bernice Manning
Southside High Scool
Newark, New Jersey

David Marshall
Rome Free Academy
Rome, Georgia

Zahra McAllister
Southwest DeKalb High School
Decatur, Georgia

Bemir Mehmedbasic
The Second High School
Sarajevo, Bosnia Herzegovina

Kristin Mercer
Milton High School
Alpharetta, Georgia

Diane Bita Minsili
College Liberman
Douala, Cameroon

Alma Mujkanovic
Prijedor, Bosnia Herzegovina

Huy D. Nguyen
Meadowcreek High School
Norcross, Georgia

Linda Norman
Americus High School
Americus, Georgia

Andy Parker
Conyers, Georgia

Jack Pepper
North Springs High School
Atlanta, Georgia

Stephanie Richey
Milton High School
Alpharetta, Georgia

Lisa Rippon
Burlington High School
Burlington, Vermont

Amy R. Ross
Open Campus High School
Norcross, Georgia

Coretia Rutledge
St. Pius X High School
Atlanta, Georgia

Manuela Saramondi
Institutio Professionale Per Il
Commercio
Brescia, Italy

Kathy Thompson
South Gwinnett High School
Snellville, Georgia

Jean C. Trent
Dunwoody High School
Dunwoody, Georgia

Dino Tufekcic
Rajac Language School
Cairo, Egypt

Marina Veal
Norcross, Georgia

Amber Walschleger
Bay City Central
Bay City, Minnesota

Melissa Watkins
South Gwinnett High School
Snellville, Georgia

Whitney Whanger
Heidelberg American High
School
Heidelberg, Germany

Jim Wilson
Sidney Lanier High School
Montgomery, Alabama

Brian Yates
Milton High School
Alpharetta, Georgia

Rosanna Yeh
Roswell High School
Roswell, Georgia

Kelly Yount
Milton High School
Alpharetta, Georgia

Kathy Zipperer
Midland High School
Midland, Minnesota